IT'LL MAKE A SPLASH

LOCH NESS

HORRIBLE GEOGRAPHY

MONSTER LAKES

ANITA GANERI ILLUSTRATED BY MIKE PHILLIPS

SCHOLASTIC

Also available
Bloomin' Rainforests • Cracking Coasts • Desperate Deserts • Earth-Shattering Earthquakes Freaky Peaks • Odious Oceans • Perishing Poles Raging Rivers • Stormy Weather • Violent Volcanoes • Wild Islands

Horrible Geography Handbooks
Planet in Peril
Wicked Weather
Wild Animals

Specials
Intrepid Explorers
Horrible Geography of the World

ISBN 978 1407 10986 2

Page layout services provided by Quadrum Solutions Ltd, Mumbai, India

Printed in the UK by CPI Bookmarque, Croydon

10 9 8 7 6 5 4 3 2

The right of Anita Ganeri and Mike Phillips to be identified as the author and illustrator of this work respectively has been asserted by them in accordance with the Copyright, Designs and Patents Act, 1988.

CONTENTS

INTRODUCTION

Everyone knows geography can be horrible. So why on Earth do geography teachers have to make it so much worse? Picture the scene. It's double geography (again) and you're getting your head down for a bit of a kip. Unfortunately, your teacher's got other terrible ideas. Next thing you know, you're standing on the shore of a dank, damp lake and it's LOATHSOME. You're up to your armpits in slimy mud and your hair's dripping with bits of waterweed. Yep, I'm sorry to say your teacher's dragged you out on another frightful field trip. How horrible is that?

To make matters worse, your teacher's droning on depressingly, even though you can't understand a word she says.

TODAY'S LESSON IS ALL ABOUT LENTIC ELLIPTICAL SINUSOIDS!

Should you call a doctor? Don't worry. It's not a nasty disease you can catch if you get wet. It's just a posh way of talking about lakes with round bottoms.

Luckily, not all geography is as deeply damp and dippy as this. Some bits are actually horribly fascinating. Yes, I know it's hard to believe. Take monster lakes, for example. Where you're going, you won't have time to worry about freezing field trips and soggy sarnies. The monster lakes in this book are among the biggest, highest, deepest and most mind-boggling places on the planet. Earth-shattering, or what? What's more, some of these loathsome lakes are so vast, murky and mysterious, they're said to be home to real-life lake monsters lurking beneath the surface. But you'll need to be feeling brave if you want to drop in for a chat.

And that's not all. From piddling ponds and paltry puddles, to large-scale lakes the size of seas, lakes and their bulging bottoms lurk all over the world. In *Monster Lakes*, you can...

• look for lakes in the tops of volcanoes

• visit an ancient underwater lake village

- find out why some leaking lakes are shrinking

- hunt for a lake monster with Blake, your monster lake guide.

Take no notice of what your teacher tells you. This is horrible geography like never before – it's awesome and out of this world. So why not take the plunge and dip into the first chapter? It's full of monster-sized facts about lakes that'll leave you shaking in your welly boots. But be warned: dabbling about in lakes can be dangerous. You never know when a miffed monster might decide to pop up and put a dampener on things.

MONSTER LAKE BOTTOMS

Close your eyes and think of a lake. Go on, don't be wet. Apart from hump-backed monsters, what do you see? You're most probably thinking of a big patch of muddy water, dotted with weedy plants and perhaps a dabbling duck or two. How boring is that? But there's much more to monster lakes than meets the eye. It's true! Ask any horrible geographer. (But brace yourself for a horribly long-winded answer. There's nothing ghastly geographers like better than the chance to show off their loathsome lake know-how.) Anyway, they'll tell you that...

TECHNICALLY SPEAKING, A LAKE IS AN INLAND ACCUMULATION OF LENTIC WATER LYING IN A DEPRESSION ON THE EARTH'S SURFACE. BLAH! BLAH! BLAH!

ZZZZ

Don't say I didn't warn you! But what on Earth is our excitable expert waffling on about? Don't worry if you don't understand a word. It's just a posh way of saying that a lake's a stretch of still water, surrounded by land, that collects in a dip in the ground. Phew! In fact, "lake" comes from an Ancient Greek word that means "hole" or "pond". But if you think that one lake looks much like another, you're wrong. Like geography teachers, lakes lurk all over the world and they're all horribly different. They range in size from

9

paltry ponds the size of bathtubs to gigantic lakes the size of whole countries. To put you in the picture, here's a map of the world's top ten monster lakes.

① **CASPIAN SEA** (378,400 sq km)
② **LAKE SUPERIOR** (82,100 sq km)
③ **LAKE VICTORIA** (62,940 sq km)
④ **LAKE HURON** (59,580 sq km)
⑤ **LAKE MICHIGAN** (57,700 sq km)
⑥ **ARAL SEA** (37,000 sq km)
⑦ **LAKE TANGANYIKA** (31,987 sq km)
⑧ **LAKE BAIKAL** (31,500 sq km)
⑨ **GREAT BEAR LAKE** (31,153 sq km)
⑩ **LAKE NYASA** (28,877 sq km)

Teacher teaser

Is your teacher keeping her head above water? Put your hand up and ask her this simple-sounding question.

PLEASE, MISS, IS THE CASPIAN SEA THE LARGEST LAKE IN THE WORLD?

GRRRR!

Does your f-laked-out teacher tell you to go jump in a lake?

Answer: The answer is yes ... and no! Strictly speaking, the Caspian Sea *is* the world's largest lake. So why on Earth is it called a sea even though it's nowhere near the coast? Good question. It's because the colossal Caspian isn't filled with fresh water. It's salty like the sea. The largest freshwater lake is Lake Superior. Drain this loathsome lake and you could cover the continents of North and South America in a knee-deep layer of water. Great news for goldfish, but depressingly damp for everyone else. In fact, Superior is so gigantic that the first Europeans who saw it thought it must be the sea. So it could have been called the Superior Sea. Confusing, or what?

THE CASPIAN IS A LAKE, SEE?

A LAKE-SEA?

Monster lake fact file

NAME: Caspian Sea

LOCATION: Central Asia

SIZE: 378,400 sq km

MAXIMUM DEPTH: 1,025 metres

MONSTER FACTS:

• Two-thirds of the Caspian Sea's water supply comes from the vulgar Volga, the longest river in Europe. Most of the rest falls as rain.

• Until about 290 million years ago, the Caspian was part of the sunny Mediterranean Sea, but then shifts in the Earth's crust blocked the lake off.

• The lake's famous for caviar. That's the posh word for sturgeon fish eggs, which are eaten as a delicacy. If you fancy a mouthful, you'll need to start saving up. A teeny teaspoonful of Caspian caviar costs a whopping £50.

• One of the lake's local names is Girkansk, which means "country of the wolves". So watch your step if you hear howling.

What on Earth are lakes?

So now you've got to know some monster lakes, but how on Earth did they get there? If you can't face another brain-numbing answer from our ancient geographer, why not dip into Blake's *Monster Lake Guidebook* instead? It gets right to the bottom of how (some of) the main lake types were formed...

Name: Glacial lakes

What they look like: Large-ish lakes and the most common kind on Earth.

Glacial lakes to check out: The Great Lakes (Canada/USA); Lake District (England); Lake Geneva (Switzerland); Hornindalsvatn (Norway).

How they happen: They form in places which, millions of years ago, were covered by gigantic slices of ice called glaciers. As the ghastly glaciers slipped and slid, they dragged along tonnes of rock, which turned them into enormous icy scouring pads. These scraped away at the ground underneath, gouging out hundreds of lake-shaped hollows. Other lakes were left behind when glaciers dumped their rocky loads at their snouts and blocked off raging rivers. (And before you turn your nose up, snout is the technical term for the end of a glacier, where the ice starts to melt.)

GLACIER

SNOUT

Sometimes blocks of ice break off glaciers and get buried under the rocks the glaciers have dumped. Years later, when the glacier is long gone, these massive ice cubes melt leaving loads of deep dips behind. The dips fill up with rain and melting snow to make lots of little lakes. Horrible geographers confusingly call them kettle lakes. Except they don't look anything like the sort of kettle you plug in to make a cup of tea. Their name comes from old-fashioned kettles, which looked like giant cooking pots. Potty.

Name: Crater lakes

What they look like: Small, deep lakes with amazingly clear, blue water.

Crater lakes to check out: Crater Lake, Oregon (USA); Lake Nyos (Cameroon); Lake Toba (Sumatra).

How they happen: They form when snow and rainfall fill the craters of steep-sided volcanoes. Volcanoes erupt when red-hot magma (that's liquid rock) spurts up through a crack in the Earth's crust (that's the Earth's rocky surface and not the crunchy bits you cut off your toast). If the magma bursts out with a bang, a violent volcano blows its top, leaving a colossal crater behind that can be tens of kilometres across.

VOLCANO → ERUPTION →

CRATER → LAKE

Crater Lake lies inside the crumbling crater of Mount Mazama. If you fancy a peak, sorry, peek, don't panic. This vile volcano last lost its cool about 7,700 years ago. But forget geography. Local legend says the eruption was caused by a battle between a brave warrior and a hot-tempered monster that smouldered away inside the mountain.

ARE YOU TALKING ABOUT ME NOW?

Nope, not yet.

Earth-shattering fact
Some lakes lie inside monster craters miles away from any fire-breathing volcanoes. So how on Earth did they get there? Amazingly, they were carved out by massive lumps of space rock called meteorites, which crashed into the Earth thousands of years ago. A smashing story.

Name: Ox-bow lakes

What they look like: Small, banana-shaped lakes.

Ox-bow lakes to check out: There are lots along the Mississippi River in the USA and the Amazon River in Brazil.

How they happen: They're made when raging rivers go round the bend. When a river flows over flat land, its flow slows along one bank and it dumps some of its load of sand and mud. But it flows faster along the other bank, wearing it away. This makes the river flow in a giant, S-shaped curve called a meander. Sometimes the roving river cuts straight across the loop, leaving behind an ox-bow lake.

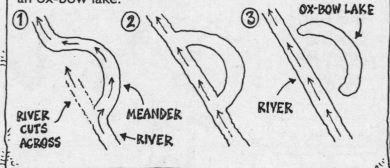

① RIVER CUTS ACROSS

② MEANDER ←RIVER

③ RIVER OX-BOW LAKE

In case you're wondering what an ox-bow is, it was a curved wooden collar worn by oxen (they're animals like very big cows) in olden times, so they could pull a plough. Bet you wish you'd never asked!

A very moving story

One man who knew more about rift valley lakes than most
was top Scottish explorer John Walter Gregory (1864–1932).
John put the Great Rift Valley in Africa well and truly on the
map. You might well ask, "What's so great about that?" but,
geographically speaking, it was no mean feat. You see, this
vast valley is actually a series of gigantic cracks running for
6,500 kilometres across Africa from the Red Sea to
Mozambique. It's 200 kilometres wide in places and the
cracks began to show about 40 million years ago.

So, although geographers had already seen it (even gormless geographers couldn't miss something that blooming big), they didn't have a clue how on Earth it had got there.

Young John was born in Scotland but went to live with his family in London. His dad was a well-off wool merchant and wanted John to follow in his footsteps. But John had other ideas. He preferred to spend his time rummaging through piles of rotten rocks or reading books about geography. Yes, I know it's horribly hard to believe. In fact, John got the nickname "Pockets" because of his horrible hobby of stuffing his pockets with lumps of rock.

Swotty John soon gave up the wool business to go off to London University. Bet he felt sheepish telling his dear old dad. Then he landed a top job at the Museum of Natural History, and it was here that he had his ground-breaking idea. He reckoned rift valleys were formed by massive earth movements. Trouble was, no one agreed with him.

At that time, most geographers blamed the wind and water for wearing rift valleys out. What John needed now was proof.

The ground under your feet looks and feels rock solid. Go on, jump up and down on it. But it's actually cracked into enormous pieces, called plates. A bit like a gigantic boiled egg you've bashed with a gigantic spoon. And get this – the plates are constantly drifting on the layer of hot, gooey rock underneath. Don't worry, you won't get carried away. They're moving so slowly, you won't notice a thing. Usually. In some places, the crazy-paving plates push and shove against each other, squeezing and squashing the rocks in between. And this is what pushes mighty mountain peaks up and sends rift valleys plummeting down.

Off to Africa

In 1892, John finally got to go to Africa to test out his crackpot theory. He set off in high spirits on an expedition across Somalia. But the journey was dreadful and John ended up falling desperately ill with a near-fatal attack of malaria (that's a deadly disease spread by mosquitoes). Even this shaky start didn't put John off though, and the following year he was back again. Stopping only to hire some local guides and buy food (a sack of veggies and a small flock of sheep), eager John set off. And this time he made some truly earth-shattering discoveries. Here's how he might have reported his finds in his postcards to his boss back home.

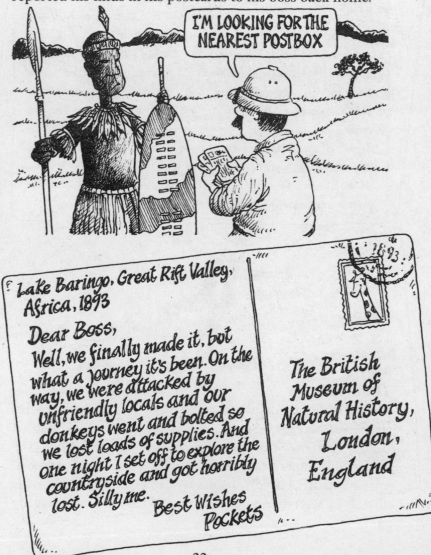

I'M LOOKING FOR THE NEAREST POSTBOX

Lake Baringo, Great Rift Valley, Africa, 1893

Dear Boss,

Well, we finally made it, but what a journey it's been. On the way, we were attacked by unfriendly locals and our donkeys went and bolted so we lost loads of supplies. And one night I set off to explore the countryside and got horribly lost. Silly me.

Best Wishes
Pockets

The British Museum of Natural History, London, England

Lake Baringo, a bit later

Dear Boss,

Luckily, there weren't any peckish lions around. To make matters worse, we ran out of water, apart from some muddy drops we found in a rhino's footprints. (Don't worry, the rhino had scarpered.) And when we finally reached a river, we had to fight off the crocodiles. Anyway, mustn't grumble. The lake's lovely and the view's breathtaking. See you soon

Pockets

The British Museum of Natural History, London, England

Lake Baringo, a bit, bit later

Dear Boss,

It's so exciting to be here at last. We pitched our tent then headed straight to the lake to reccy the rocks around the shore. I'm sure the way the rock layers are arranged will prove how the valley's slumped... Guess what?

I was right all along. But you'll need to use your imagination for this next bit. The countryside around here's like a giant chunk of cake with layers of yummy sponge, cream and jam.

More to follow... all the best

Pockets

The British Museum of Natural History, London, England

Lake Baringo - a bit, bit, bit later

Dear Boss,

Are you with me so far about the giant chunk of cake? If you cut the chunk into three smaller slices and try to pick it up, the middle bit will slip down. Yes, I know it makes a mess. And that's (almost) how a rift valley forms. Only here the layers are made of rock. The drifting plates of the Earth's crust shifts at faults (giant cracks in the crust). This causes the slab of rock in between to sink, leaving a vast, steep-sided valley behind.

A perfect place for lakes.

Best wishes Pockets

The British
Museum of
Natural
History,
London,
England

Lake Baringo - a bit, bit, bit, bit later

Dear Boss.

I've scribbled down a handy diagram for you to chew over. Go on - it's a piece of cake.

COUNTRYSIDE

LAYERS
OF ROCKS

FAULT LINES

ROCK SINKS
DOWN

The British
Museum of
Natural
History,
London,
England

Right, I'm off for lunch. All this talk of cake is making me hungry.

see you soon Pockets

The two sides of the Great Rift Valley in Africa are still d-rifting. Experts think it'll eventually crack up completely and split Africa in two. But not for another ten million years. Then the loathsome lakes that lie in the bottom will become an odious ocean.

Back home, John wrote two books and hundreds of serious scientific papers about his adventures, and became professor of geology at Glasgow University. He even had a bit of the Great Rift Valley named after him. But his story had a very sad ending so I hope you've got a hanky handy. In 1932 he went to Peru in South America to do some more exploring and was killed when his canoe capsized. How unlucky was that? But having pockets full of rocks probably meant it was easier to sink than swim.

ALL VERY FASCINATING BUT IS IT MY TURN NOW?

Er, no, not yet.

Horrible Health Warning

If you're looking for a lake to lurk by, you might want to give Lake Vostok in Antarctica a miss. For a start, this far-away lake lies under 4 kilometres of ice. So you'd need a satellite out in space to spot it. From satellite photos already snapped, scientists have sussed out that vast Lake Vostok's almost as big as Lake Ontario, one of the Great Lakes. And it's at least half a million years old. Excited scientists reckon there are bacteria living in the lake that have never been seen before. They still don't know how these deep-freeze bacteria can survive in the ice-cold water. But they're hoping to get to the bottom of things by drilling a hole through the ice and sending a roving robot down.

Congratulations! You've survived your d–icey lake visit without even getting your feet wet. If you're not careful, you'll be calling yourself a limnologist soon. Don't worry, it's got nothing to do with arms and legs. A limnologist is a horrible scientist who studies swamps and lakes. The word was coined by a Swiss swamp scientist who made the first in-depth study of lakes in 1892. He started his study with loathsome lake water. And luckily that's what the next chapter is all about. Time to take the plunge.

STILL WATERS

Ask your teacher what feature all lakes share and she'll probably try to boggle your mind with lots of baffling lacustrine* facts. No wonder you've got that sinking feeling. But you can ignore everything she says. (Oh, so you do that already?) The simple truth is that all lakes are full of water. OK, so you don't need to be a genius geographer to work that out. Some lakes are filled with fresh water and some are salty like the sea. But compared to the amount of water in the salty sea, lakes are just a drop in the, er, ocean.

Note: *Sorry, she's started already. Lacustrine simply means anything to do with lakes.

Earth-shattering fact
Everyone knows that counting sheep is supposed to send you off to sheep, sorry, sleep. But if you fancy a bit of shut-eye, why not try counting monster lakes instead? So far, horrible geographers have notched up over a million, so it's no wonder they're always nodding off. Zzzzzzz. Sorry, where was I? Even though they get everywhere, lakes contain less than 0.017 per cent of the Earth's water supply. (Most of the rest – about 97 per cent – is salty and lies in the oceans and seas. The rest is fresh but it's frozen solid in glaciers and ice caps, or flows in rivers or underground.) 0.017 per cent sounds like a minuscule amount, doesn't it? But get this – it's still enough wonderful water to fill 74 BILLION (a billion's a thousand million) OLYMPIC-SIZED SWIMMING POOLS! Talk about making a splash...

A watery end

But where on Earth did all this water come from? And how did it end up slopping about in lakes? Here's a monster-sized fact for you to impress your friends with. The water lapping in lakes today has sloshed millions and millions of times before. It's recycled again and again in the water cycle. So the water in the gigantic Great Lakes may once have been a dippy dinosaur's paddling pool. Pretty amazing, eh?

But if the only sort of cycle you know is the one you pedal to the shops, don't worry. Who better to help you get a grip on things than Blake's very own Uncle Pete, the plumber. He's been fitting water systems like this for years, and he's brought a horribly useful diagram along.

Mornin' folks, Pete the plumber here. I hear you're having a spot of bother with your water cycle. I don't want to put a spanner in the waterworks but it's a tricky bit of kit to install. Get some of this perishing pipework wrong and you could end up in very deep water indeed. Never mind — stick with me and we'll soon have it going again.

1 First, you need to make sure your sun's shining in the right place so it heats your water up. Over the oceans is spot on.

2 When it's nice and warm, some of your water will turn into water vapour (technically speaking, we plumbers call this evaporation).

3 Your warmed-up water vapour should rise into the air. (You'll have to take my word for this — water vapour's invisible.) As it rises, it'll cool down and turn back into droplets of liquid water (called condensation in the trade). Shout if I'm going too fast.

4 Next, you want to get your water droplets to gang together to make a cloud. Don't skimp on your droplets, mind. You'll need millions of these beauties to make this bit work properly.

RAIN CLOUD

LAKE

RIVER

5 Inside the cloud, you want your droplets to bash into one another. Then they'll make drops that are too heavy to hang around and they'll eventually fall as rain. Don't worry, your clouds haven't sprung a leak so you can put your spanner away.

6 If your clouds are working properly, some of the rain will fall back into the sea or soak into the ground. But you should have plenty left to keep your lake nice and full. It might splash straight into your lake or into a river that'll pipe it into your lake.

Pete's Top Tip

Look after your water cycle and you'll get years of wear out of it. The great thing is that once you get it up and running, it keeps working over and over again. Without you having to do a thing! This model's still going strong and it's been working for millions of years. Right, I'm off to fix some batty old boiler that's on the blink again.

WHO ARE YOU CALLING AN OLD BOILER?

The ins and outs of leaky lake water
• *THE INS…*

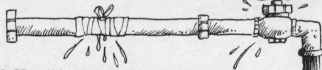

1 Horrible geographers now know that water gets into lakes in different ways. Some rain and snow falls straight into lakes from clouds. Yep, it's really as simple as that. This can mean massive amounts of water for lakes like vast Lake Victoria in Africa. It gets two thirds of its total water supply from rain. That's billions and billions of buckets full.

2 Some water leaks into lakes from melting snow and glaciers high up on mountainsides. The Great Lakes in North America get almost half their water like this (see page 97 for more Great Lake facts). And there's a handy knock-on effect, because the water flows from Lake Superior to fill up Lake Michigan and Lake Huron. (There are actually five Great Lakes but they're also all joined up.) But if the year's snowfall is on the low side, lake-water levels fall alarmingly.

3 Gallons of water gushes up into lakes from underground. This is called groundwater and it happens when rain soaks through the rocks and soil. We're not talking little drips either. There's nearly 40 times as much water washing away under your feet as there is in all of the world's rivers and lakes. That's seriously soggy stuff. Luckily, lakes don't only depend on groundwater to fill them up. If they did, they'd be in for a horribly long wait. Sluggish groundwater flows so slowly it can take thousands of years to surface again.

4 For years, horrible geographers didn't know that groundwater could seep straight up through a lake bed. It was just a wild guess. But in 1974, some curious Canadian scientists decided to get to the bottom of things. Here's what they did. They injected the ground around Perch Lake in Canada with salty water. Later they tested the water lying on the lake bed. What do you think they found?

a) The lake water was no saltier than before.

b) The lake water was much saltier.

c) The lake water turned mouldy and green.

Answer: b) The salty solution had soaked through the rocks and seeped into the lake water. So you could say the scientists' needle-sharp experiment had proved their point.

5 Where do many raging rivers end up? In monster lakes, that's where. Rivers pour running water into lakes all over the world. In fact, some lakes have not just one but hundreds of rivers keeping them nice and wet. Rivers rush awesome amounts of water into Lake Tanganyika in Africa. And get this – if the rivers cut off their water supply, the lake would take a staggering 1,200 years to dry up because it's so blooming big.

AND THE OUTS…

1 You might think that lakes just sit there, sloshing gently to and fro. But scratch beneath the surface and you'll find lakes are constantly springing leaks. Some water's washed away by rushing rivers and streams. (Sounds horribly draining.) But is it really so straightforward? The answer is, yes… Except when a river changes course and starts flowing backwards instead! This is what happens to the Tonle Sap (Great Lake) in Cambodia. The lake's drained by a river, also called the Tonle Sap, which flows into the mighty River Mekong. During the dry season, the lake shrinks to about 2,500–3,000 square kilometres. Then things take a very strange turn. In the rainy season, the meek-looking Mekong turns into a raging torrent. It races into the Tonle Sap River in such a rush that it forces the river to change direction and flow back into the lake again. And before you can say "Go jump in a lake", the lake's flooded to five times the size.

2 Some lakes simply dry up in the sun. Take Lake Eyre, for example. It's the largest lake in seriously sunny Australia, measuring a massive 9,300 square kilometres. This enormous salt lake's named after British explorer John Eyre (1815–1901), who spotted it in 1840. But instead of meeting a watery end, exhausted Eyre nearly died of thirst. You see, the lake lies in the middle of the desperate desert and it's usually as dry as a bone. What happens is this. In the baking hot weather, any rain evaporates (turns to water vapour) so quickly that most of the rivers running into the lake dry up before they reach it. In fact, it rains so rarely, the dried-up lake only fills up ONCE EVERY 50 YEARS!

3 Salt lakes are salty because, well, they've got so much salt in them. Obviously. Just like the stuff you shake all over your chips. Some of this comes from volcanoes or underground springs. Some falls in rain or snow. But most of it comes from rocks on land and is washed into the lake by the rain and rivers. If the lake is located in a warm place, evaporation helps, too. As the water evaporates in the sun, it leaves the salt behind and over time the lake gets saltier and saltier. And evaporation sucks up water from the soil.

In a salty water competition, the Dead Sea in Israel would easily win first prize. This loathsome lake is a staggering eight times saltier than the sea. So why on Earth is it so blooming salty? For a start, the lake gets its water supply from the River Jordan, but the river's being rerouted to provide water for farming so less water's reaching the lake and it's shrinking. And less water means the water that's left is even saltier. That's because the lake's in such a hot-spot; temperatures in summer can reach a boiling 54°C. Phew! In this sweltering heat, the water in the lake evaporates horribly quickly, leaving a thick, salty soup behind. No wonder the Dead Sea is so, er, deadly that almost nothing can live in it for long. But the salt also makes the water dead easy to float in, so if you fancy a dip, you won't need your rubber ring. You can even read a newspaper while you're floating along. But keep your head above water so the salt doesn't sting your eyes.

YOUR DRINK, SIR

4 Loads of lake water drains away into the ground. It seeps into cracks in limestone rock and ever-so slowly eats it away, carving out underground tunnels and caves. Some of it may trickle down into underground rivers which flow into underground lakes. Trouble is, these secretive lakes are

buried hundreds of metres below the ground, so unless you've got X-ray vision, they're horribly hard to spot. Or unless, like our next intrepid explorer, you're happy to find yourself in a very deep hole. Are you ready to meet him?

ARE YOU TALKING ABOUT ME?

Don't worry, it'll be your turn soon.

Deep, dark and down under

Even as a boy, adventurous Edouard-Alfred Martel (1859–1938) was so keen on caves that he spent all his spare time rootling about underground. Well, it beats collecting stamps or knitting socks for a hobby, I suppose. Edouard-Alfred was born in France. At school, he was brilliant at geography but later he got a job as a lawyer like his dad. So did he forget all about caves? No way. In his summer holidays, he and his companions explored caves all over Europe. You can hear the rest in Edouard-Alfred's own words. We found this in-depth interview in an old copy of the *Daily Globe* when our reporter caught up with Ed between dips, sorry, trips.

HE THINKS HE'S A MOLE!

When did you start getting interested in caves?

When I was seven years old. My dad took me to a cave in Belgium. It had a huge lake in the bottom and I knew at once I wanted to be a cave explorer when I grew up.

So why did you become a lawyer instead?

I needed the money, but the work really got me down. My real love was always caves. After work and in the holidays, you couldn't keep my feet on the ground.

I see. And what sort of caving kit do you take with you?

A couple of rope ladders, a winch, some lamps and my trusty collapsible canoe.

Is that all?

Well, I also wear a special pair of overalls which I designed myself. I'm quite proud of them, actually. They've got pockets for everything — whistle, candles, matches, hammer, knives, tape measure, thermometers, pencils, notebook, compass, walkie-talkie, and first-aid kit, of course. I also pop in a bottle of rum and a couple of bars of choccie in case I get peckish.

With that lot to lug about, I'm surprised you can squeeze into a cave. How do you do it?

It's easy, really. First, I find a pothole (that's a hole leading underground). Then I chuck a cannon ball down it, tied to a rope. That tells me how long my rope ladder needs to be. You don't want to be left dangling in mid-air, do you?

No, I suppose not. What happens next?

Then we rig up a wooden frame over the pothole and fix the winch and ropes to it. Usually I climb down the ladder. But sometimes I sit on a plank and get lowered down on a rope. It's OK unless the rope starts spinning. That makes you feel dizzy and sick.

Sounds horrible. What was your most dangerous moment?

Oh, there have been so many, I don't know where to begin. Once, two friends and I were paddling across an underground lake when we bashed our heads on a low piece of rock. We were all knocked into the water and our candles went out so we couldn't see a thing. I hadn't a clue where I was. (And I'm scared of the dark.) Then my wet clothes started to drag me down and I began to panic. Luckily, my friends managed to pull me out. Just in time. Any longer in the icy water and I'd have drowned or frozen to death. Oh, and once a candle set fire to my hair while I was dangling on the end of a rope. That was a hairy moment, but I wasn't going to cave in.

> *Gulp! And what was your greatest discovery?*

It's got to be the Lac de la Chapelle in France. It's an underground lake I stumbled across in 1889. From the surface, there wasn't much to look at – just a gaping hole in a field. But underground, it was a different story. What a fantastique place! A network of winding tunnels and rivers leading into vast chasms and caves. A-maze-ing. I'll never forget my first sight of the lake. We'd been paddling down a river that was so narrow in places we had to carry the canoe on our heads and wade through the water. The rocks were horribly slimy and we kept losing our footing. Then the river seemed to disappear. All that was left was a narrow tunnel barely half a metre high. It was a tight squeeze, I can tell you. But somehow we managed to wriggle through ... into a towering chamber containing a huge, shimmering lake. It was like a fairyland. Sadly, we couldn't stay long. We were dripping wet by then and we'd nearly run out of candles. Besides, it was almost dinner time.

Did you ever go back to the lake?

Ah yes, many times. And we've even put in a staircase and electric lights in case people don't fancy swinging down on a rope. Legend says there's a stash of gold hidden down there so we've had plenty of visitors. Would you like to buy a ticket for the boat?

Er, no, thanks. I think I'll give it a miss. So where are you off to next?

Oh, back underground, of course. There's a couple of caves in England I'd like to have a crack at. If you're passing, make sure you drop in, won't you?

By the time he died in 1938, busy Edouard-Alfred had explored a ground-breaking 1,500 caves and underground lakes. Hundreds of these had never been seen before. Back home, he found time to write for a scientific journal and became professor of underground geography at the Sorbonne University in Paris. He even set up a brand-new society for speleologists (that was the brand-new name for scientists who study caves).

Teacher teaser

Is your clever-clogs teacher clued-up about the ins and outs of lakes? Or is his lake know-how leakier than a sieve? Why not ask him this draining question:

How often do lakes change their water?
a) Every five days.
b) Every year.
c) Every 700 years.

I COULD DO WITH A CHANGE!

Answer: It doesn't matter which answer he picks because all three are true! Lakes regularly replace their old water. But how quickly they do it depends on how fast water flows in and out. Marion Lake in Canada is super speedy, with a change of water every five days. Mirror Lake in the USA is less than a tenth of the size of Marion Lake, but it's much deeper so its water takes a year to replace. Lagging well behind is Lake Tahoe in the USA. To swim in fresh lake water, you'd have to wait for a staggering 700 years.

Lake life cycles

Lakes do funny things to people. Some people only have to glimpse a lake and they go all giggly and gooey-eyed. Some even start writing soppy poetry like *"Nothing so fair, so pure, and at the same time so large, as a lake, lies on the surface of the Earth"*. Revolting but true. (This particularly pathetic piece was penned by the American poet Henry David Thoreau in the 19th century.)

But if you're one of those people who think lakes are as dull as ditchwater, here's something to cheer you up. Lakes don't hang around for ever. Over time, they turn into dreadfully dry land.

Some lakes can be destroyed overnight by violent volcanic eruptions or earth-shattering earthquakes. Others get dumped on by rockfalls or avalanches, sand and dust, or simply dry up in the sun. But for most lakes, it's a much more slow-moving story. Here's what happens:

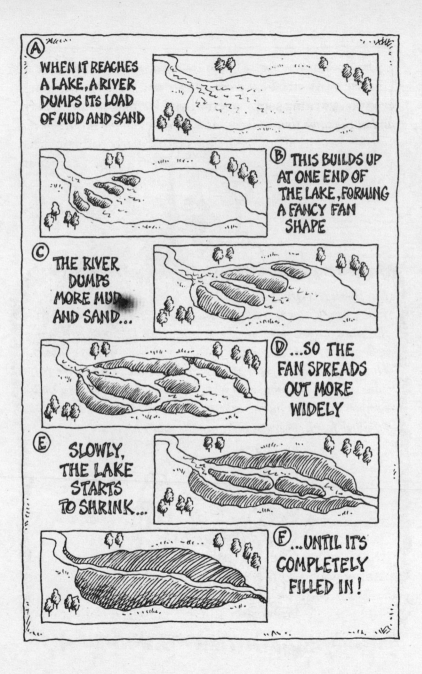

A WHEN IT REACHES A LAKE, A RIVER DUMPS ITS LOAD OF MUD AND SAND

B THIS BUILDS UP AT ONE END OF THE LAKE, FORMING A FANCY FAN SHAPE

C THE RIVER DUMPS MORE MUD AND SAND...

D ...SO THE FAN SPREADS OUT MORE WIDELY

E SLOWLY, THE LAKE STARTS TO SHRINK...

F ...UNTIL IT'S COMPLETELY FILLED IN!

The good news for all you budding poets is that it takes most lakes millions of years to dry up, so you've got plenty of time to get scribbling.

Earth-shattering fact
Vast Lake Victoria is about twice the size of Belgium and is the third-largest lake in the world. But 13,500 years ago, believe it or not, this gigantic lake was bone-dry grassland. How on Earth do geographers know about that? After all, none of them are quite that old. The answer is that they took samples of mud from the lake bottom and found it was full of fabulous fossils of grassland animals and plants.

But you don't need to scrape the bottom to meet some loathsome lake wildlife. You just need to turn the page. Lakes are perfect hiding places for plants and animals like flighty flamingos, fancy fish and beetles that go round and round in circles.

MONSTER LAKE WILDLIFE

Lakes may look damp and depressing – hardly the sort of places you'd want to hang around in for long, especially when you could be back in your nice, dry home, vegging out on the sofa. But despite the water-logged conditions, a monster number of plants and animals think lake-living is the lap of luxury. Even so, setting up home in a loathsome lake's not as straightforward as it seems. It pays to pick which bit of a lake to live in before you go wading in. Don't want to risk getting your own feet wet? Why not send Blake instead? He's already wearing his diving gear.

ON THE EDGE
The bit around the lake edges where the water laps on to the shore. It's packed with plants like reeds and rushes, which make the perfect hiding place if you're a fish or a water bird. Trouble is, the wind can make the water quite choppy so you might feel a bit seasick.

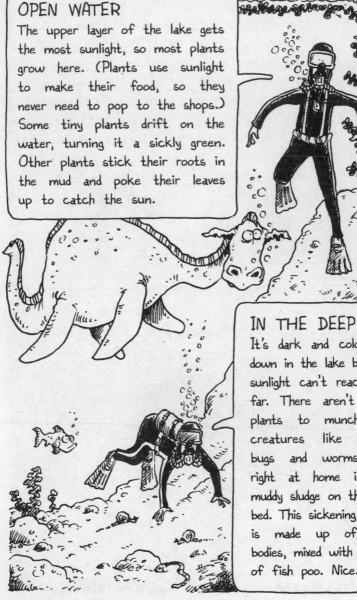

OPEN WATER

The upper layer of the lake gets the most sunlight, so most plants grow here. (Plants use sunlight to make their food, so they never need to pop to the shops.) Some tiny plants drift on the water, turning it a sickly green. Other plants stick their roots in the mud and poke their leaves up to catch the sun.

IN THE DEEP

It's dark and cold deep down in the lake because sunlight can't reach this far. There aren't many plants to munch but creatures like snails, bugs and worms feel right at home in the muddy sludge on the lake bed. This sickening sludge is made up of dead bodies, mixed with dollops of fish poo. Nice.

Earth-shattering fact

Millions of puny plants called algae float on the lake surface. But never mind blooming pot plants and fragrant flowers, most of these piddling plants are so tiny you'd need a microscope to see them at all. Size isn't everything, though. Without this vital veg, nothing could live in lakes. For a start, they make oxygen, which all lake animals need to breathe. And they're also on the menu for lunch. They're scoffed by small lake creatures like shrimps and water fleas, and they're scoffed by bigger creatures like fish and frogs, and they're scoffed by even bigger fish and creatures like herons and crocs. You get the idea.

SO WHERE DO I FIT IN?

Sink or swim?

Imagine you've been dragged off on another horrible geography field trip. (Don't panic – this time it's not for real.) Which of the things on this list do you think you wouldn't be able to live without?

a) Food to eat.

b) Oxygen to breathe.

c) A way of getting about.

d) A safe place to hide.

The answer is you need all of them. Especially the safe place to hide if your teacher's in a monster bad mood. Amazingly, they are exactly the same things lake-loving animals need to survive. So how on Earth do they do it? Well, the creepy-crawlies you're about to meet have special features to help them cope. Some of them are weirder than others. Why not find out more with this f-lakey lake quiz? If you think a creature feature is false, answer SINK! If you think it's true, answer SWIM! Yep, it really is a cut-and-dried case.

1 Great diving beetles can't swim. SINK OR SWIM?

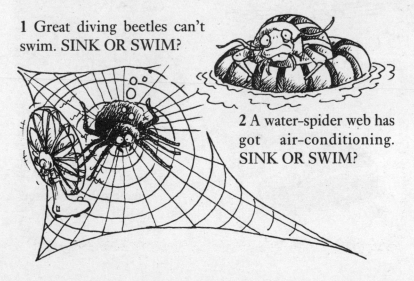

2 A water-spider web has got air-conditioning. SINK OR SWIM?

3 Water scorpions use snorkels to breathe. SINK OR SWIM?

4 Caddis fly larvae live in tents. SINK OR SWIM?

5 Horse leeches eat horses. SINK OR SWIM?

6 Pond skaters wear tiny waterskis. SINK OR SWIM?

7 Lake limpets cling on to rocks with their feet. SINK OR SWIM?

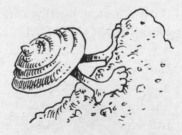

8 Whirligig beetles wear goggles for seeing under water. SINK OR SWIM?

Answers:

1 SINK! Great diving beetles are born swimmers with bodies brilliantly designed for the job. They're sleek and streamlined for cutting through water and their back legs work like tiny oars. But forget beetling about leisurely, these boating beetles zoom along at top speed looking for tadpoles, insects and fish for lunch.

2 SWIM! The water spider spends most of its life under water in a web spun between strands of waterweed. But it needs to breathe oxygen from the air, so it regularly swims to the surface and traps big bubbles of air on its hairy back. Then it uses the bubbles to air-condition its watery web. Pretty clever, eh?

3 SWIM! Water scorpions are sluggish bugs that like to lurk in shallow lake bottoms. They get their name from their long tails, but these scorpions' tails don't pack a painful sting. Instead, a water scorpion climbs up a plant stem, sticks the tip of its tail out of the water, and uses it like a snorkel to suck in air.

4 SWIM! OK, so they're not the sort of tents you'd go camping in. Caddis fly larvae, or bugs, crawl along the lake bottom, looking for bits of dead leaves to crunch. To avoid ending up as another animal's dinner, they build themselves little tents from bits of snail shell, stones and grains of sand, glued together with slimy spit.

5 SINK! Of course they don't, silly. For a start, these clinging creatures are just 6 centimetres long – that's about the same as your little finger. And besides, they like to swallow their prey whole. So they'd never be able to

open their mouths wide enough to fit a whole horse in. Instead, they scoff much smaller fry like worms, snails, tadpoles and rotten fish. Phwoar!

6 SINK! Pond skaters don't actually wear waterskis, but they can walk on water without sinking. How on Earth do they do it? Well, the surface of water's covered in a fine, springy film or skin, strong enough to stand a pond-skater's weight. The pond-skater has got special hairs and claws on its feet for gripping the skin without breaking it. These busy bugs dash across the surface, grabbing dead insects to eat.

The technical name for the watery skin is surface tension. Of course, it's not real skin like the stuff that covers your body and gets scratched when you fall off your bike. It's actually made from very tightly packed water molecules. (Molecules are joined-up atoms, and atoms are the minute objects that make up all substances.) Sounds horribly technical, but it really works. Try this tense experiment to test it out.

What you need:
• A bowl
• Some water
• Some blotting paper*
• A paper clip*

What you do:
1 Fill the bowl with water. Pretend this is a lake.
2 Float the blotting paper on the water with the paper clip on top.
3 Wait for the blotting paper to go soggy and sink.
4 The paper clip should stay in place because surface tension holds it up. (By the way, the paper sinks because it soaks up water and gets too heavy to stay on the surface. The paper clip stays put because it's so light and the film holds it up.)

* If you've got a pet pond-skater, you can use that instead. But don't put a paper clip on top.

7 SWIM! Lake limpets live on wind-swept lake shores where it's horribly easy to get carried away. But lake limpets have a shore, sorry, sure-footed way of coping. They graze on algae growing on rocks and stones, and use their broad feet to hang on for dear life. For an even more watertight fit, the edges of their shells are soft and squishy for squashing into cracks in the rocks.

8 SINK! Whirligig beetles don't wear goggles, but they do have an eye-catching way of seeing where they're going. These busy bugs spend most of their lives whirling about on the water surface like a bunch of mini dodgem cars, looking for insects for tea. But they quickly dive under water if they're in danger of being gobbled up first. So it's just as well their eyes are divided in two for looking up and down at the same time. Eye, eye.

Fancy lake fishing

You've probably heard the saying, "There are plenty more fish in the sea." It's the sort of dreadfully drippy thing grown-ups say to make them sound cleverer than they actually are. Take no notice. If it's fancy fish you're after, forget the sea and look in a lake instead. Fancy stocking your lake with fabulous fish that'll turn your friends green with envy? But are you in a flap about which fish to pick? Why not drop into Uncle Fin's Fancy Fish Shop for some expert fish-keeping tips? Like Uncle Fin, you'll soon be well and truly hooked.

FISH? GRRR! WHO WANTS FISH WHEN YOU COULD HAVE A MONSTER INSTEAD?

Don't panic, we're getting to you.

Welcome to my Fancy Fish Shop. Glad you could drop in. If it's fish you fancy, you've come to the right plaice, sorry, place. But you won't be needing that bowl. It might be OK for a goldfish but it's about as much use for these freaky fish as a shoebox for an elephant.

A smashing fish, this one, if you don't mind its horrible habits. For a start, it doesn't send its kids to nursery. A mother cichlid lays her eggs, then scoops them up into ... her mouth. She can't eat or swallow for days in case she gulps them down by mistake. When the baby fish hatch, they stay in their mouthy house until they're about a week old. Then their miffed mother spits her fishy mouthful out and heads off to stuff her face. If you're thinking of keeping a cichlid, stock up on algae, shellfish and sponges for them to eat. That's the sea creatures, not the stodgy cakes your dear old granny makes.

NAME:
CURIOUS CICHLID
WHERE IT LIVES:
NORTH AMERICA, AFRICA
SIZE: **UP TO 75 cm LONG**

NAME: **LOOPY LUNGFISH**
WHERE IT LIVES: **EAST AND CENTRAL AFRICA**
SIZE: **2 METRES LONG**

OK so it won't win any beauty contests but this fella's horribly hardy. In the wet season, when there's plenty of water, it lives just like a normal fish and breathes through gills (they're slits on the sides of its head that take in oxygen dissolved in the water). The trouble starts when the weather changes and its lake and oxygen supply dry up in the sun, leaving the lungfish high and dry. But not for long. This feisty fish digs a burrow in the damp mud, slips into it like a slimy sleeping bag (it stops its skin drying out) and snoozes until it rains again. Which might be months or even years. Until then, it breathes through two pouches which work a bit like lungs.

A bit of a slippery character this one, but don't let that put you off. Tenches are horribly useful if you happen to cut yourself. Forget sticking plasters – a tench's slimy skin is supposed to have healing properties. So all you need to do is catch a tench and rub it on your wound. An old wives' tale, if you ask me. If you're off tench fishing, wait for nightfall. Tenches spend the day slumbering in the shade but come out at night to scoff snails and shellfish.

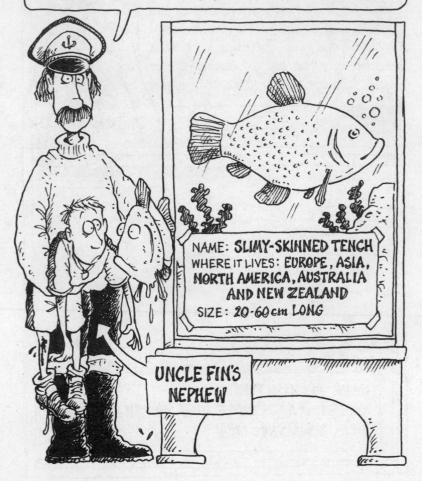

NAME: **SLIMY-SKINNED TENCH**
WHERE IT LIVES: **EUROPE, ASIA, NORTH AMERICA, AUSTRALIA AND NEW ZEALAND**
SIZE: **20-60 cm LONG**

UNCLE FIN'S NEPHEW

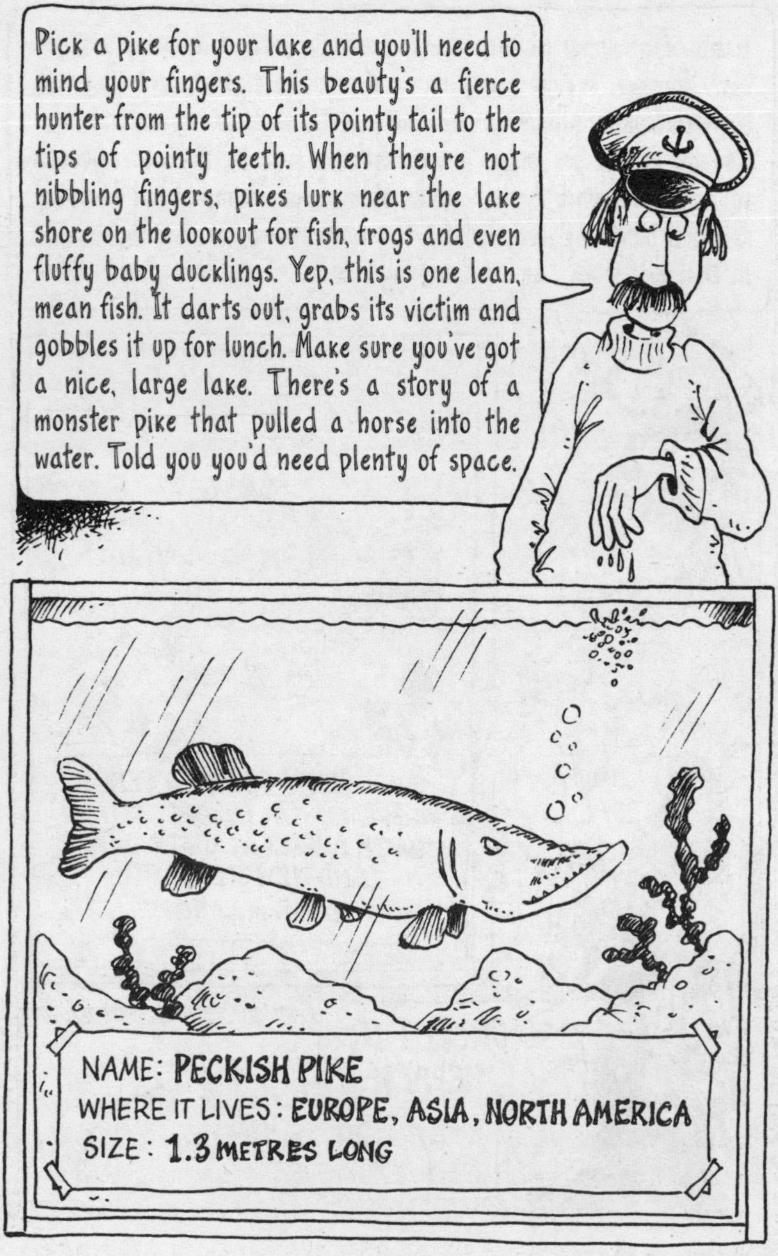

Pick a pike for your lake and you'll need to mind your fingers. This beauty's a fierce hunter from the tip of its pointy tail to the tips of pointy teeth. When they're not nibbling fingers, pikes lurk near the lake shore on the lookout for fish, frogs and even fluffy baby ducklings. Yep, this is one lean, mean fish. It darts out, grabs its victim and gobbles it up for lunch. Make sure you've got a nice, large lake. There's a story of a monster pike that pulled a horse into the water. Told you you'd need plenty of space.

NAME: **PECKISH PIKE**

WHERE IT LIVES: **EUROPE, ASIA, NORTH AMERICA**

SIZE: **1.3 METRES LONG**

If you fancy one of these fish, you'll have to hurry while stocks last. You see, they're horribly hard to come by because they live over a kilometre down in the depths of Lake Baikal. And nowhere else on Earth. That far down, the pressure of the water would squash you flat, but the gutsy golomyanka swims about happily. A third of this freaky fish's body is made up of oil, which helps it stay afloat in the f-f-freezing cold water. At night, it swims up to the surface to find crayfish to crunch. But it can't stay for long. If it gets too warm, it melts in the sun, leaving only its old bones behind!

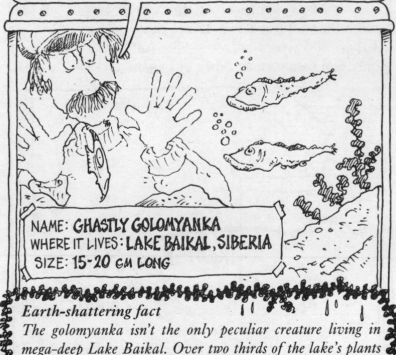

NAME: **GHASTLY GOLOMYANKA**
WHERE IT LIVES: **LAKE BAIKAL, SIBERIA**
SIZE: **15-20 CM LONG**

Earth-shattering fact
The golomyanka isn't the only peculiar creature living in mega-deep Lake Baikal. Over two thirds of the lake's plants and animals are found NOWHERE ELSE! They include the neatly named nerpa, the world's only freshwater seal. And the nerdy nerpa's favourite food is ... deep-fried golomyanka.

Monster lake fact file

NAME: Lake Baikal

LOCATION: Siberia

SIZE: 31,500 sq km

MAXIMUM DEPTH: 1,620 metres

MONSTER FACTS:

• Record-breaking Baikal is about 25 million years old, making it the oldest lake on Earth.

• It's also the deepest lake. It would easily wash over five Eiffel Towers perched on top of one another.

• It contains a fifth of all the world's fresh water, more than all five Great Lakes put together.

• Over 300 rivers keep the lake full to the brim, but only one paltry river flows out again.

Blake's waterbird-watching tour

If you thought monster lake living was plain sailing, you'd be wrong. Dead wrong. Especially if the lake you choose to live in is a sinister soda* lake. Apart from the suffocating heat, bitter water and stinking mud, you'll need to cope with your lake drying up. Then you'll be stranded on a cracked crust of soda like the icing on a gigantic birthday cake. But this is no place for a picnic. In some parts, the soda's so thick you could drive a truck over it. But woe betide you if you fall in – the soda will burn you alive.

* Important note: The technical name for soda is sodium carbonate. It's salt-like stuff used to make glass, soap and detergents (that's things like washing powder). In small quantities, it's harmless to humans and brilliant at getting your clothes clean.

Surely these hostile conditions are too harsh for any animal to handle? Well, incredibly they aren't. One particularly plucky bird is perfectly suited to life on these lethal lakes. Can you guess what it is? Here's a clue. This bird-brain is always in the pink. Got it yet? It's the fabulous flamingo, of course. Now I know what you're thinking. Flamingos are all pink and fluffy — how could these fragile-looking birds possibly survive? The truth is that these amazingly adaptable birds are as tough as old boots. Forget boring budgies. Flamingos are my favourite birds. And I've travelled all the way to Lake Nakuru in Kenya to watch them in the wild. Ooh, goody, there's one over there...

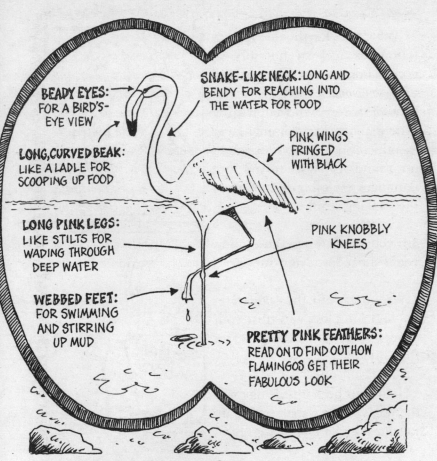

BEADY EYES: FOR A BIRD'S-EYE VIEW

SNAKE-LIKE NECK: LONG AND BENDY FOR REACHING INTO THE WATER FOR FOOD

LONG, CURVED BEAK: LIKE A LADLE FOR SCOOPING UP FOOD

PINK WINGS FRINGED WITH BLACK

LONG PINK LEGS: LIKE STILTS FOR WADING THROUGH DEEP WATER

PINK KNOBBLY KNEES

WEBBED FEET: FOR SWIMMING AND STIRRING UP MUD

PRETTY PINK FEATHERS: READ ON TO FIND OUT HOW FLAMINGOS GET THEIR FABULOUS LOOK

Some flighty flamingo facts

1 Fancy flamingo-watching? Head for the Great Rift Valley in Africa and you won't be able to miss them. In particular, sweltering Lakes Nakuru, Natron and Magadi are worth watching. Over half the world's flamingos live here in huge flocks tens of thousands of birds strong. Burning soda washes into these loathsome lakes from nearby volcanoes or bubbles up in boiling underwater springs. So get ready for a red-hot ride.

2 Why on Earth do flighty flamingos feel so horribly at home? Because the lakes are full of their favourite food, that's why. Blooming algae and squirming little water shrimps simmer away in a thick, soda soup. This might not sound very tasty to you, but flamingos can't guzzle enough of the stinking stuff.

3 If you're a flamingo, here's how you'd slurp down your supper:

• Wade out into the lake water on your long legs and turn your head upside down. It's trickier than it looks.

• Hold your beak upside down in the water so the water reaches up to your nostrils.

• Now sweep your head from side to side. Mind you don't lose your balance.

• Use your tongue to suck in water, then pump the water out again. The bristly edges of your beak work like a sieve to sift out mouthfuls of lovely grub.

Warning: if you're not a flamingo, don't try this out at home. Especially if your posh aunty's coming round for tea. Use a soup spoon instead.

4 With all that nourishing food to feast on, it's no wonder flamingos are in the pink. Red colouring in the plants and shrimps turns the flamingos' feathers a fabulous bright pink. Very pretty. (By the way, this colouring is the same stuff that gives carrots their carroty colour.) Without it, the birds' feathers soon fade to a shade of dirty grey and they can't breed properly. You'd think having bright-pink feathers might make you easier for enemies to spot. But fashion-conscious flamingos couldn't care less. They live in such a hostile habitat that other creatures don't bother dropping in for lunch.

carrots

5 When the time comes to build a nest, flamingo parents pick a spot on the crusty lake shore – even though the levels of soda would be lethal to most other creatures. They use their beaks to squirt and squash lumps of mud into a mound shape, then scoop out the top like an egg cup. The nest is about 30 centimetres tall so it doesn't get flooded by scalding lake water and the egg doesn't get hard boiled. Both parents take turns to sit on the egg until it hatches.

6 With its grubby grey feathers and boring straight beak, a newly hatched flamingo chick doesn't look much like its mum and dad. It stays in the nest for about two weeks, gulping down bright-red milk sicked up by its parents. Fancy a glassful?

Horrible Health Warning
For Scottish scientist Leslie Brown, a flamingo-watching trip nearly proved fatal. In the 1950s, he set off to look for flamingo nests around Lake Natron – on foot! It was a dreadful journey. Armed only with a bottle of water, he started walking across the scorching soda crust. Trouble is, the crust kept cracking, leaving him knee-deep in stinking black mud. Every step was horribly hard but he dare not stop in case he sank. But worse was to come. When he took a sip of water, he found the soda had made it too bitter to drink. Almost dead on his feet, Leslie decided to give up and started the long slog back to base, even though it was now the hottest part of the day. What a nightmare! Desperately thirsty and bitterly disappointed, he could only manage five or six steps at a time before collapsing with exhaustion. Against all the odds, Leslie staggered home safe and sound, but he knew he was lucky to be alive. His feet were so badly burned by the soda that he had to spend weeks in hospital. But even that didn't put flamingo-mad Leslie off. Incredibly, a year or two later, he was back at Lake Natron again.

SODA MUCH FOR FLAMINGOS!

But don't think flighty flamingos, slimy-skinned tench and scuba-diving spiders are the only water-logged wildlife you'll find lurking around lakes. While you're busy stocking up on crayfish for your ghastly golomyanka's tea, be careful you don't stumble across the weirdest lake animals of all. What are these mysterious creatures? Yep, you've guessed it. They're horrible humans and they keep popping up everywhere.

HANG ON, WHAT ABOUT ME?

It'll be your turn soon. Honest.

MONSTER LAKE LIVING

You might think living by a lake sounds about as exciting as catching a cold. Luckily, millions of people around the world aren't as pathetically weedy as you. So why on Earth do so many horrible humans call monster lakes home? What do lakes have to offer that you can't get on dry land? Well, for a start, lakes are horribly important for humans. And I don't just mean for the lovely views. They are so important that people have been living around them for centuries. We'll be back after this commercial break...

REED, RUSH & DUCKWEED
ESTATE AGENTS

FOR SALE

OODLES OF OLDE-WORLDE CHARM

IT'S THE LAP OF LUXURY!

SUPERB LOCATION IN A SCOTTISH LOCH

ONE HOUSE WITH STUNNING PANORAMIC LAKE VIEWS. BUILT OF TOP-QUALITY WOOD, STONES AND EARTH. PLENTY OF STORAGE SPACE AND ROOM FOR ANIMALS ON THE GROUND FLOOR.

SPECIAL FEATURES

WE CALL THIS MODEL THE "CRANNOG" (THAT'S SCOTTISH FOR "TREE") BUT YOU CAN CHANGE THE NAME OF YOUR TREEHOUSE IF YOU LIKE. AND YOU WON'T NEED A BURGLAR ALARM. FOR SAFETY, THE HOUSE IS BUILT ON A WOODEN ISLAND RIGHT IN THE MIDDLE OF THE LAKE. BUT DON'T WORRY, IT WON'T FLOAT AWAY. IT'S HELD IN PLACE BY STONES AND WOODEN STAKES DRIVEN DEEP INTO THE LAKE-BED MUD.

SMALL PRINT: WE THINK THE HOUSE IS ABOUT 3,000 YEARS OLD SO EXPECT SOME WEAR AND TEAR. AND IT'S BEEN UNDER WATER FOR CENTURIES, SO IT COULD BE QUITE DAMP. IT WAS ONCE ABOVE WATER BUT AS THE LAKE LEVEL ROSE, IT SANK. SO YOU'LL NEED A BOAT TO REACH IT - AND SOME DIVING GEAR!

SPECIAL OFFER

ARRANGE TO VIEW YOUR CRANNOG TODAY AND WE'LL THROW IN A FREE BUTTERDISH. IT'S EXACTLY LIKE THE ONE FOUND IN A CRANNOG IN LOCH TAY IN SCOTLAND, PERFECTLY PRESERVED BY THE PEATY WATER. IT EVEN HAD SCRAPS OF BUTTER STUCK TO IT - BUT

FREE

THIS BITTER BUTTER WAS 2,500 YEARS OLD SO IT HAD STARTED TO WHIFF HORRIBLY. GO ON, LET US BUTTER YOU UP A BIT!

OTHER LAKE LOCATIONS TO CHECK OUT:

LAKE ZURICH - SWITZERLAND:

IN THE 1850s THE REMAINS OF AN ANCIENT WOODEN VILLAGE WERE FOUND POKING OUT OF THE MUDDY LAKE BED. THE VILLAGE WAS ORIGINALLY BUILT ON THE SHORE OF THE LAKE, BUT AS THE WATER LEVEL ROSE, IT WENT UNDER FAST.

Lake living – the monster truth

Still got that sinking feeling? Can't wait to get back to dry land? Before you ditch the idea of lake living, here's something that might change your mind. Even the dampest, most dismal lakes have their uses. It's true. Here are five sure-fire reasons for setting up home near a lake.

1 Refreshing fresh water

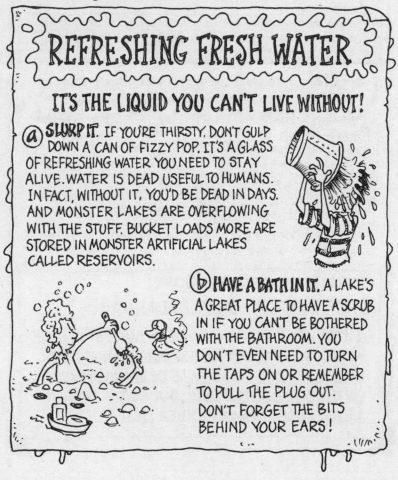

REFRESHING FRESH WATER

IT'S THE LIQUID YOU CAN'T LIVE WITHOUT!

ⓐ **SLURP IT.** IF YOU'RE THIRSTY, DON'T GULP DOWN A CAN OF FIZZY POP. IT'S A GLASS OF REFRESHING WATER YOU NEED TO STAY ALIVE. WATER IS DEAD USEFUL TO HUMANS. IN FACT, WITHOUT IT, YOU'D BE DEAD IN DAYS. AND MONSTER LAKES ARE OVERFLOWING WITH THE STUFF. BUCKET LOADS MORE ARE STORED IN MONSTER ARTIFICIAL LAKES CALLED RESERVOIRS.

ⓑ **HAVE A BATH IN IT.** A LAKE'S A GREAT PLACE TO HAVE A SCRUB IN IF YOU CAN'T BE BOTHERED WITH THE BATHROOM. YOU DON'T EVEN NEED TO TURN THE TAPS ON OR REMEMBER TO PULL THE PLUG OUT. DON'T FORGET THE BITS BEHIND YOUR EARS!

ⓒ WATER YOUR CROPS WITH IT.

PUMP WATER FROM THE LAKE AND SPRINKLE IT ON YOUR FIELDS. TECHNICALLY, THIS IS CALLED IRRIGATION BUT WATERING MEANS THE SAME THING. ALL THIS WATER WILL MAKE YOUR CROPS GROW NICE AND HEALTHY. ESPECIALLY RICE, WHICH LOVES BEING WATERLOGGED.

ⓓ FUEL YOUR FACTORY WITH IT.

FACTORIES USE MONSTER AMOUNTS OF LAKE WATER TO TURN RAW MATERIALS LIKE STEEL INTO CARS. AND WITH THE LAKE ON YOUR DOORSTEP, YOU'VE GOT A HANDY WAY OF MOVING YOUR GOODS ABOUT.

ⓔ LIGHT YOUR HOME WITH IT.

USE YOUR LAKE TO MAKE ELECTRICITY. BUILD A DAM ACROSS ONE OF THE RAGING RIVERS FLOWING INTO OR OUT OF YOUR LAKE. AS THE WATER FLOWS THROUGH THE DAM, IT TURNS THE BLADES OF A WHEEL CALLED A TURBINE. IN TURN, IT DRIVES A SHAFT WHICH DRIVES A GENERATOR WHICH MAKES ELECTRICITY. SHOCKINGLY SIMPLE.

WHIRL!

Earth-shattering fact

Thousands of years ago, green-fingered Ancient Egyptian farmers grew their crops in the crumbly black soil left behind when the River Nile flooded. Ah yes, those were the days. But they wouldn't be able to do it today. In the 1960s the awesomely high Aswan Dam was built across the river – blocking off a monster reservoir called Lake Nasser. This lake's so enormous it can hold twice the yearly flow of the Nile. Which is good news for modern Egyptians, who have a steady supply of water for drinking, irrigation and generating electricity. But here's the catch. The lake's already leaking alarmingly, and it's getting horribly clogged up with mud and pebbles washed in by the river. But that's not all. Building the dam was disastrous for tens of thousands of local people whose homes were flooded and destroyed. And it's goodbye fertile farmland as the Nile Delta (that's where the river flows into the sea) shrinks dramatically. What's more, an ancient temple had to be chopped into hundreds of pieces and rebuilt on top of a cliff. Bet the Ancient Egyptians would have been pretty cut up about that.

2 Mouth-watering food. Many lake-loving humans make their living by fishing. Fish are also vitally important for food. They're packed with healthy proteins and vitamins and are delicious with salad or chips. Time to get your teeth into these fishy facts.

• Remember Tonle Sap in Cambodia? An astonishing four million people rely on the lake for their food and livelihoods. Fishermen catch about 23,000 tonnes of lake fish a year. That's an awful lot of fish. Many fishermen actually live on the lake with their families, in floating houses made from bamboo. How would you like that? Don't worry, you wouldn't have to miss school. There are also floating shops, doctors' clinics, temples and ... classrooms.

• The Turkana people from Lake Turkana in Africa didn't start off as fishermen. For centuries, they lived as nomads (people who move from place to place in search of food and water), looking after their herds of goats, cattle and camels. But after a dreadful drought, they gave up their wandering lifestyles and turned to fishing instead. Trouble is, the lake now seems to be shrinking and less water means fewer fish to catch. So it looks as if the lives of the long-suffering Turkana are set to change all over again.

• Billions of buzzing brine flies live on the shores of Lake Mono in the USA. (In fact, Mono means brine fly in the local Indian language. And yes, I know it's not strictly a kind of fish.) This loathsome lake is THREE TIMES SALTIER than the odious Atlantic Ocean. The brine flies lay their eggs on the lake shore and the eggs hatch into little wriggling grubs. Years ago, the local people used to collect them for food. They dried the gruesome grubs in the sun then made them into a ready-salted soup. Fancy a mouthful?

3 Time-saving transport. Forget getting stuck in traffic jams or missing the bus. With a lake on your doorstep, getting from A to B is a doddle. Though you'll need to get yourself a boat. Take your pick from a simple canoe (for short journeys) to a paddle-steamer (for a longer, more luxurious trip). Or you might be better off with a barge if you've got loads of goods to lug around.

People have been using lakes to get about for centuries. Why? Well, apart from being horribly handy, going by lake is usually quicker than legging it overland. So which route are you going to take? What about sailing the St Lawrence Seaway? It's over 2,000 kilometres long and links the Great Lakes to the Atlantic Ocean. Each year, millions of tonnes of coal, iron, grain and timber are shipped to and fro along the seaway. But choose your departure date carefully. The seaway's open from April to December, for the rest of the year it's choked with ice.

4 Odious lake oil. Oodles of the oil we use comes from under the sea, but there may be oodles more oozing away under monster lakes. And it's horribly valuable. To find out how on Earth it got there, you have to go back millions of years to the time when lakes were full of tiny prehistoric plants and animals. When they died, their bodies sank to the lake bed and were squashed under layers of rock.

OIL IS NOT WELL!

Ever-so slowly, they turned into thick, gungy oil. You'd have to dig deep to get the oil out – if you can find it, that is. There may be 200 billion barrels of oil glugging around under the Caspian Sea. And it's worth a small fortune. Trouble is, the countries around the lake are still squabbling about who all this valuable oil belongs to. Sp-oil sports.

HORRIBLE HOLIDAYS ARE PROUD TO PRESENT THEIR LATEST, ACTION-PACKED ADVENTURE

WELCOME TO

MONSTER LAKE WATER WORLD

FOR A HOLIDAY THAT'LL MAKE A SPLASH!

> SMALL PRINT: WE CAN'T GUARANTEE YOUR SAFETY. IF YOU FALL IN, DON'T BLAME US. ESPECIALLY IF YOU CAN'T SWIM.

ICE-YACHTING

Forget boring yachting on water. Wait until the lake freezes over and try a spot of ice-yachting instead. Ice-yachts (like windsurfers on skates) will be provided. If the wind's right, you'll whizz along at speeds of up to 160 km/h, though we can't guarantee it. And your ice-yacht doesn't have brakes so when you want to stop, simply steer straight into the wind. If the ice breaks and you fall, stay with your boat, whatever you do. A set of bear claws will come handy. Don't worry, they're not joined on to a bear. They're actually ice picks for hauling you back on to the ice. Right, who's having the first go?

SHIPWRECK SPOTTING

Learn how to use sonar to track down a shipwreck. (Flick forward to page 105 for the low-down on sonar.) There are thousands of rotting wrecks lying on lonely lake beds around the world. A good place to start shipwreck-spotting is the spookily named Shipwreck Coast off Lake Superior. Over 4,000 weed-covered wrecks have already been found, but there are loads more left for you to spot.

SCUBA DIVING

Dive into the lake water and come face-to-face with thousands of fabulous lake creatures. If you haven't got your own diving gear, you can hire it from our diving school shop. For beginners, Lake Malawi is a good place to pick. The water is beautifully clear and warm, and the sandy bottom makes for a lovely soft landing (if you don't mind the fish poo). Besides, some 1,500 species of fish live in this lovely lake so you'll have plenty to look at. And please don't worry about crocodiles. They stick to slow-moving rivers. Usually.

LAKE CRUISING

OK, time to take things easy with a lazy lake cruise. Why not hop on board our luxury liner and take a tour of all five Great Lakes? You can sail all the way from Chicago to Toronto on our eight-night cruise. The ship's equipped with a swimming pool, hair-dressing salon, restaurants, library and gym if you get bored of the lovely lake views. There's even a hospital in case you feel seasick. Of course, all this luxury doesn't come cheap and this exciting excursion will set you back an extra £2,500.

TODAY'S SPECIAL OFFER:

If you like life in the fast lane, race a high-speed vehicle across a dried-up lake bed. These bone-dry lakes are called "playas", from a Spanish word for beach. But you can leave your bucket and spade at home. You'll be reaching speeds of over 950 km/h, so you won't have time to build sandcastles. Playas are so pancake flat they're often used for testing high-speed cars, setting speed records and even landing spacecraft.

A NOTE FROM YOUR HOLIDAY COMPANY

To do most of these activities, you need to be fabulously fit and strong (and filthy rich). Drippy types should try our much less daring Wet Weekend Break instead. There's plenty to keep you busy — like pond dipping or picking waterweeds. Yawn.

Teacher teaser

Want to get up your teacher's nose? Why not ask her this bloomin' lovely question? It's not to be sniffed at.

"Please, Miss, where do carnations* come from?"

a) A carnation farm.
b) An African lake.
c) Your grandad's flower bed.

* Carnations are pretty pink or white flowers, in case you were wondering. If you want to make your teacher go all gooey-eyed, why not buy her a nice big bunch?

AAARHH! I'M ALLERGIC TO FLOWERS!

Answer: b) 200 million carnations are grown each year along the shores of sunny Lake Naivasha in Africa. You'd need a monster-sized vase for a bunch that big. They're watered by SEVEN MILLION TONNES of water piped out of the lake. Chemicals are also sprinkled on to the fields to make the soil richer. Which is great news for blooming flowers, but geographers are worried the chemicals are poisoning the lake.

Monster lake lifestyles

As you know, monster lakes pop up all over the world, which means there's an awesome variety of lake lifestyles. Some lakes are so remote that people still live almost the same way they've lived for centuries. Other lakes have big, bustling, modern cities on their shores and are homes to millions of lake-dwellers. Looking for a relaxing lakeside break? Unsure about which lake to pick? We sent Blake to check out two top lakes and find out how people live there. Here's his roving report...

Everything about Lake Michigan is mind-bogglingly big and brash. For a start, it measures a massive 58,000 square kilometres, making it the USA's biggest lake and the third-largest Great Lake. Even its name means "big water" in the local Indian language. Some really big, brash rivers flow into the lake, and the Chicago River was once one of them. But in the early 1900s, a series of artificial rivers and canals was built to force the river to flow the other way! This helped to stop disease-causing sewage flowing into the city's drinking water, which came from the lake. Even the cities on the shores of the lake are monstrously big and brash. I'm here in seriously high-tech Chicago.

Talk about action-packed. Three million people live in this bustling city and it's one of the world's top centres for industry and transport. So it's no wonder Chicago's one of the busiest ports on the lake, shipping goods all over the USA. But despite all the hustle and bustle, Chicago is a mega-cool place to hang out. Here's a piccie of me taking a break on one of the lakeside beaches. (This chilled-out city has got 46 kilometres of lake front.) Have a nice day!

I've hopped south to Lake Titicaca for a peek at a very different lake lifestyle. This monster lake lies high up in the Andes Mountains, miles from anywhere. The local Uru people have lived on the lake for years, but they don't have mod cons like running water, telephones or electricity. They live quite traditionally. Take boat-building, for example. They make their banana-shaped fishing boats from bundles of totora reeds, which grow in the lake shallows. A boat takes about two weeks to make and lasts for about six months. Then the reeds start going rotten and the boat's likely to get waterlogged and sink.

But that's not all these rotten reeds are really useful for. You can burn them for fuel, feed them to pigs, make them into baskets and rope, and even clean your teeth with them. What's more, the Uru build floating reed islands in the lake where they live in reed huts and keep their pigs in little floating reed pig pens. And if you've got tummy ache, a nice cup of totora flower tea will soon have you feeling better.

P.S. The local Uru people have lived on the lake for centuries, but today their lives are changing. Most of their meals are made up of fish (together with some pork from their pigs) and potatoes. But the lake's being horribly polluted by waste from the towns and cities growing up around the shore. And this pollution is poisoning the fish – and the Uru people who eat them. If the lakeside cities don't clean up their act, the Uru's ancient lifestyle might disappear. And that would be a terrible tragedy.

Monster lake fact file

NAME: Lake Titicaca
LOCATION: Peru/Bolivia
SIZE: 8,300 sq km
MAXIMUM DEPTH: 270 metres
MONSTER FACTS:

• It's 3,812 metres above sea level, making it the highest navigable lake on Earth (that means the highest lake you can sail on).

• It's got 25 rivers flowing into it, but only the Desaguadero River flows out. This raging river then flows into Lake Poopo (it's true) in Bolivia.

• Its name means "rock of the puma" because the lake is said to be shaped like a puma playing with a rotten rock.

• Legend says the ancestors of the Incas (the ancient people of the region) were sent down to Earth by the sun to live on an island in the lake.

Lethal lakes

Deadly poisonous fish aren't the only horrible hazard lurking in monster lakes. For the people of Nyos in Cameroon, lakeside living turned into a terrifying nightmare...

THE DAILY GLOBE

22 AUGUST 1986

NYOS, CAMEROON, WEST AFRICA

The stunned residents of Nyos are today reeling from the worst tragedy to hit the town in years. As night fell, a cloud of toxic gas from nearby Lake Nyos rolled silently down the hillside into the valley, suffocating 1,700 people.

Most people died in their beds. Shocked survivors told how they saw others drop down dead in the middle of talking or eating. The trouble was, apart from the sound of a small explosion, there had been no warning of the danger ahead. The killer gas was mostly deadly carbon dioxide, undetectable because it has no smell.

Leaky crater lake

The source of the killer gas was Lake Nyos, a small, deep lake, formed inside the crater of a volcano. The lake looked harmless enough, with its clear blue water and cornfields on its grassy shores. But beneath the surface, disaster was brewing. For hundreds of years, poisonous gas had been leaking from the volcano and collecting in the water at the bottom of the lake. Experts think a small earthquake, strong winds or a landslide may have stirred the water up … triggering the release of the deadly gas. But no one knows for sure.

Cattle killer

For now, the handful of survivors are counting the cost of last night's fateful events. Many have already fled their homes, too terrified to live by the lake for a moment longer. Others have lost everything they own. Hadari, a cattle-herder, tried to find the words to describe the devastation the gas had caused. "I live with my family on the hillside above the lake," he told our reporter. "We were woken up by a low rumbling noise. We saw the gas pour down the valley like a river of smoke. We climbed higher up the hill and hoped we'd be safe there. I know we're lucky to be alive, but we've lost all our cattle and our living. I don't know what we're going to do now."

Tragically, 21 August was market day so herders from miles around had brought their cattle to Nyos to sell. Just in time to be caught in the killer gas's path. By morning, the fields around the town were littered with the bodies of thousands of cattle. Eerily, no flies or vultures hovered around the corpses as they usually would. There were simply none of them left alive.

Plugging the leak

Since that dreadful August night, more murderous gases have been building up in the depths of the lake, turning it into a terrifying time bomb. Scientists have been working against the clock to make sure the lake doesn't kill again. But how on Earth can the lethal leak be plugged? The scientists hope they've found the answer. They've sunk a long, plastic pipe into the lake so the end dangles just above the lake bottom. The idea is to suck the gas-rich water up so it gushes up gently like a fountain. Then the gas can escape harmlessly into the atmosphere rather than going off with a bang. They've also installed an early-warning system, so if the levels of gas rise dangerously it sets off a series of sirens and strobe lights. And the local people can get outta there – fast.

Are these measures working? Or are they just a pipe-dream? The truth is it's too early to tell for sure. But scientists are pleased with what's happened so far. Trouble is, there's so much ghastly gas left in the lake, they'd need four or five more pipes to suck it all out, and funds for the project are running out. But at least for the traumatized people of Nyos, the nightmare's over – for now.

MONSTER LAKE EXPLORATION

Forget tedious trips to the seaside. Wave bye-bye to boring caravan holidays. For the adventure of a lifetime, why not explore a monster lake? You'll be following in the footsteps of some amazingly intrepid explorers. Why on Earth did they pick up sticks and set off? Well, some of them were hoping to make their fortune and went in search of goods to trade. Others wanted to get from A to B and stumbled across lakes accidentally. And others simply wanted to see the world. Of course, they didn't all become dead famous. In fact, some of them ended up in very hot water indeed. Got the guts to join them? Go on, don't be a drip. But you'd better get a move on, or you'll miss the blooming boat.

RIGHT, I'VE HAD ENOUGH OF THIS. IF IT'S NOT MY TURN SOON, I'M OFF HOME!

You might want to hang around for a bit longer.

LOCH NESS

LAKE TITICACA

CASPIAN SEA

Ace 16th-century Spanish explorer Antonio de Sepulveda couldn't care less about geography. He was after gold and legend said that Lake Guatavita in Colombia was crammed full of the shiny stuff. In ancient times, a sparkling ceremony took place on the lake. The local king paddled out into the middle with a priceless cargo of gold and precious stones. Then he chucked the whole lot overboard as an offering to the gods. But how on Earth could gold-digging de Sepulveda get his greedy mitts on this sunken loot? Simple. He got 8,000 workmen to cut an enormous notch in the rim of the lake and let the water flow out. Did his potty plan work? Astonishingly, it did. All that draining left the lake 20 metres lower and Antonio managed to salvage armloads of glittering gold jewellery and a gorgeous emerald the size of an egg. Bet he was egg-static about that.

Going fur-ther

Believe it or not, our next bunch of globetrotters stumbled across the gigantic Great Lakes in North America ... while they were looking for something else. What was this long-lost something? Cute, furry creatures, that's what! Warning: we'd like to apologize to all you nature-loving readers out there. This furry tale is about to turn nasty and you might want to skip the next bit. You see, these lake-hoppers were after valuable animal furs to buy and sell back home. It was particularly bad luck for beavers. Their costly fur was in such demand for making furry hats and coats the beavers were nearly wiped out. For fur-ther details about the frightful fur trade, why not pay a visit to the newly opened Horrible Geography: Fur-trappers' Rogues' Gallery? Blake's ready to give you a guided tour.

Sam's dad was a sailor, so young Sam had exploring in his blood. By the time he was 25, he'd already sailed as far as South America and back. But he didn't stop there. In 1603, salty sea-dog Sam left his home in France for Canada and sailed up the St Lawrence River, where he stumbled upon Lakes Ontario and Erie. (He later also reached Lake Huron.) Though he didn't realize they were lakes at first. He thought these whopping stretches of water meant he'd reached the odious ocean. Far-sighted Sam's real job was to track down a top spot for a French fur-trading post. But he spent his spare time lake-hopping and making maps of the places he paddled past. What's more, he went on to write four best-selling geography books. What a guy!

SAMUEL DE CHAMPLAIN
(1567-1635)
NATIONALITY: FRENCH

ETIENNE BRULE
(AROUND 1592 – 1633)
NATIONALITY: FRENCH

At the tender age of 16, young Etienne sailed to Canada to work for Sam de Champlain. No sooner had he landed than his boss sent him to live with the local Algonquin Indians, and he learned to speak their language. This came in horribly handy later on when Etienne helped guide Sam on his epic journey to Lake Ontario. But that's not all intrepid Etienne was good for. He also knew how to make an Indian birch-bark canoe and where to find food in the woods. Later, Etienne went back to visit the locals and ended up spending another 18 years with them. He travelled thousands of miles with them and became the first outsider ever to spot Lake Superior. Unfortunately, well-travelled Etienne met a grisly end. His friends accused him of spying and boiled him and ate him for lunch! Bet he was as tough as old boots.

Like unfortunate Etienne, Jean Nicolet spent years living like a local. In fact, he spoke the local lingo so fluently that Sam de Champlain (again) gave him a job as his interpreter (that's someone who translates words from one language into another). But Jean's finest moment came in 1634. Sam sent him on an expedition to Lake Huron to make peace between two warring tribes. He also hoped Jean would be able to find a brand-new river route to the Pacific Ocean. With seven local guides and a large canoe, daring Jean set off. He didn't look much like an explorer. For travelling, he wore a long silk robe, embroidered with brightly coloured birds and flowers. Pretty over-the-top. The locals were so gobsmacked, they stopped fighting at once. Nattily dressed Nicolet didn't find his passage to the Pacific, but he did go on to discover mammoth Lake Michigan.

JEAN NICOLET (1598-1642)
NATIONALITY: FRENCH

Rene-Robert trained to be a priest but he turned his back on the Church and ran off to sea instead. In 1666, he sailed to Canada and made pots of dosh as a fur-trader. But he wasn't ready to settle down yet. Nope, restless Rene-Robert had horribly itchy feet and couldn't wait to head off on a great lake-hopping trip. So he built himself a fine boat called the Griffon and sailed across Lakes Erie and Huron. After that, he paddled across Lake Michigan in a canoe. Just for the fun of it. Then disaster struck. The gorgeous Griffon sank, along with its costly cargo of furs. Poor Rene-Robert reached rock bottom, but he wasn't downhearted for long. Soon he was off on his travels again and became the first European to canoe down the Mississippi River from the Great Lakes to the Gulf of Mexico. An astonishing feat for the time. But his story has a sad ending. In 1687, some of his men rebelled and one of them shot him dead. Sniff!

RENE-ROBERT DE LA SALLE
(1643-1687)
NATIONALITY: FRENCH

* Important note: in case you hadn't noticed, all the fur-trappers in the Hall of Fame were French. Oh, you knew that already? This wasn't simply because the fashionable French were particularly fond of wearing fur, but because French fur-trappers were the first Europeans to settle in Canada and they claimed the lands they discovered for France. Unfortunately, many of these lands already belonged to the local Indians. Thousands of them were killed, forced to flee from their homes or died from deadly diseases caught from the French and other settlers.

Monster lake fact file

NAME: The Great Lakes (Superior, Michigan, Huron, Erie and Ontario)
LOCATION: Canada/USA
SIZE: 245,660 sq km (total area)
MAXIMUM DEPTH: 405 metres
(Lake Superior)
MONSTER FACTS:

• They were carved out by gigantic glaciers that started melting about 18,000 years ago. Lake Erie is the oldest Great Lake at the grand old age of about 10,000 years.

• Lake Superior is the biggest Great Lake and the largest freshwater lake in the world.

• The smallest Great Lake is Lake Ontario. It's about a quarter of monster Lake Superior's size.

• Four Great Lakes – Superior, Huron, Erie and Ontario – form the boggy border between the USA and Canada. All of Lake Michigan lies in the USA.

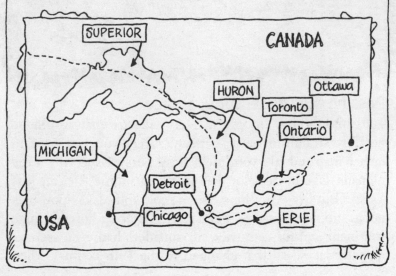

American Peter Pond (1740–1807) was an explorer who really lived up to his name. Pete's dad was a shoemaker and Pete had seven little brothers and sisters. No wonder he couldn't wait to leave home. In 1778, he set up a trading post near Lake Athabasca in chilly north-west Canada and made his fortune in furs. Pretty soon, though, Pete was bitten by the lake-hopping bug. On his travels, he canoed down the Clearwater River and paddled across the Great Slave Lake. And woe betide anyone who got in his way. He was famous for his terrible temper and had already been accused of murder – twice. In fact, Pete wasn't involved in either of them, but he lost his job anyway and was sent home in disgrace.

Passing the sauce, sorry, source

You might think finding a likely lake to visit would be horribly straightforward. I mean, surely you just have to open a map and take your pick? Easy, peasy. Especially if the monster lake in question lies in the awesome African Rift Valley? But like everything else in geography, lake-spotting's not as simple as it seems. For a start, Africa's a horribly huge continent and for centuries, no outsiders had even seen its monster lakes. All that changed in the 19th century when some incredibly intrepid explorers from Europe set off for Africa. (Of course, local people had known about these lakes for years.) These hardy travellers weren't actually looking for lakes at all. They'd set their sights on finding the long-lost source* of the River Nile.

* The source is the place where a raging river begins. It's nothing to do with the gloopy red stuff you dollop on your sausage sandwich. The source of a river may be a glacier, a mountain stream or even a leaky lake.

Many top geographers tried (and failed) to find the secret source, including hardy husband–and–wife team, Samuel and Florence Baker. They'd fallen in love at first sight when Sam spotted Flo on sale in a slave-market in Bulgaria. Soppy, or what? From then on, they were never apart. Here's how re-source-ful Florence might have described their African adventure in her secret diary (if she'd kept a diary, that is).

June 1862, Khartoum, Sudan

At last! After a whole year in Africa we've finally reached Khartoum. I can't believe it's taken so long. It took ages to cross the desert from Cairo (I never ever want to see a camel again!) and we also stopped off to learn Arabic so we could chat to the locals. I'm quite fluent in it now. But what an appalling place this is. Luckily, we're not here for long. Sam's just been sent a letter from London asking us to take supplies to Gondoroko, about 1,500 kilometres to the south. From there, we can finally start our search for the source of the Nile. Yippee! Now I've got to find boats (and boatmen), horses, donkeys, armed guards and supplies for the next four months. All by myself. Sam's gone elephant hunting (again) with a local bigwig, leaving me to sort everything out. Grrrr.

February 1863, Gondoroko, Africa

We arrived here by boat a week ago. And this place is even worse than Khartoum. It's horribly hot and smelly, and there are mosquitoes and flies everywhere. Not to mention rats the size of cats. Oh, and one of our guides was shot dead. Even Sam's finding it hard to keep smiling and he's always horribly cheerful. Anyway, we got to meet Sam's old friends Grant* and Speke* at last (that's who the supplies are for). They'd just returned from a trip up river and had some news for us. Bad news, I'm sorry to say. They claimed they'd already found the source of the Nile at Lake Victoria. As you can imagine, Sam was bitterly disappointed. I've never seen him so upset. But he perked up when Speke told him there's another large lake left to discover that might also feed the river. Grant even drew us a map. But they warned us it'd be a long, hard slog, not suitable for a lady. Pah! I'll show them.

That's top British explorers James Augustus Grant (1827–1892) and John Hanning Speke (1827–1864). Like the intrepid Bakers, they spent years searching for the Nile's long-lost source.

January 1864, Bunyoro Kingdom

It's taken almost a year to get here and what a dreadful journey it's been. Most of our guides scarpered so we had to hitch a lift with some slave traders (and you know how I hate slave traders). And the weather's been awful. We couldn't move for months on end because the rivers were too full to cross. Half of the animals dropped down dead, and we had to eat grass when our food ran out. To make matters worse, Sam and I fell sick with a terrible fever. What a nightmare! Finally, a few weeks ago, we were on the move again and soon reached Bunyoro.

The king's a bit of an oddball, to say the least. We gave him loads of pressies (shawls, shoes, necklaces, rifles and even a Persian carpet), but he still wasn't satisfied. Get this. He wanted Sam to leave me behind while Sam went to look for the lake.

Sam was furious and threatened to shoot the king on the spot. My hero! Things looked as if they might turn nasty but Sam offered the king his tartan kilt (yep, he'd lugged it all the way from England) and his best compass instead. Luckily, the king agreed. So we're just about to set off. I can't wait to get outta here...

14 March 1864, Lake Albert, Uganda/Congo

We've made it! We've finally made it and I can't believe I'm still here to write this diary. We travelled for miles and miles every day, through the terrible, choking heat. At one point, Sam felt so woefully weak he went and fell off his ox. (He was OK apart from a few nasty bruises and his wounded pride.) But I was so ill for days and days that Sam decided I was dead and started to dig my grave! Luckily, I opened my eyes just in time, otherwise he'd have had me buried alive! But none of that matters now. After months of hardship, we've finally reached the lake. And what a beautiful sight it is. A glittering sea of water, stretching as far as the eye can see. Sam's already named it Lake Albert (after Queen Victoria's dead hubby). A lovely touch. He's sure it's the real source of the Nile, whatever old Grant and Speke say. Right, I'm off for a lovely, long dip.

A tale of two lakes

Unfortunately for long-suffering Sam and Flo, Speke turned out to have been right all along. The source of the River Nile was a river flowing out of Lake Victoria. Very annoying. It's true that the Nile flows at one end of Lake Albert, but it runs into the lake, not out of it. Despite their disappointment, the trailblazing Bakers put Lake Albert (the seventh-largest lake in Africa) well and truly on the map and earned their place in the geography books. Back home, they were treated like superstars and Sam was made a knight. (But first they got married.)

Modern monster lake explorers

Still feeling amazingly bold and adventurous? Still keen to push the boat out? If all this talk of lake-hopping has given you horribly itchy feet (and your socks are clean on), you're in luck. But you'll need to be feeling brave. Modern lake exploration is no wild goose chase. For a start, the creature you'll be looking for is a lot more mysterious than any gormless goose. Yep, you've guessed it. You're going lake-monster hunting. Don't worry, your teeth will stop ch-ch-chattering once you get moving.

Are you brave enough to launch your own monster hunt?

Step 1: Pick your lake

It may be the most famous but Loch Ness isn't the only lake where monsters are thought to lurk. Scratch the surface and you'll find sightings of similar creatures in hundreds of lakes all over the world. Take Lake Champlain in the USA, for example. (It's named after, yes, you've guessed it, ace explorer Samuel de Champlain, who discovered it in 1609.) Stories of a lake monster go back hundreds of years. Nicknamed "Champ", it's described as having a long, snaky neck and several hard-to-miss humps on its back. But if you don't get to see Champ, never mind. You can always tuck into some scrummy "Champ's chips" (made to a secret recipe) or tune in to Champ 101.3 FM, the monster's very own radio station, instead.

Other lake monsters to check out: Ogopogo (Lake Okanagan, Canada); Issie (Lake Ikeda, Japan).

DID SOMEONE SAY CHIPS?

Step 2: Stock up on monster-hunting equipment

If you're going monster-hunting, it pays to have the right gear. But be warned: some of it's horribly pricey so you'll need to start saving up. If you think you can afford it, here's some of the equipment you'll need:

• A boat: you'll be spending hours out on the lake so make sure your boat's got lots of mod cons.

• A sonar machine: expensive but essential for tracking the monster down. Buy a model you can tow alongside your boat. Sonar uses sound to detect underwater objects like shoals of fish, whales and, er, monsters. It's already been used to find the wreck of the *Titanic*. So you'd think finding a monster would be a walk in the park. Here's a quick guide to how to use your sonar machine.

1 The sonar machine sends out a high-pitched PING (too high for your ears to hear).

2 The sound waves hit an object in the water…

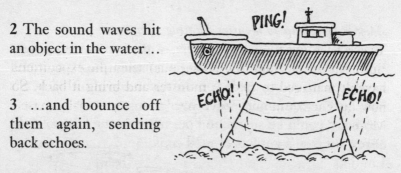

3 …and bounce off them again, sending back echoes.

4 The machine works out how far away the object is…

5 …and shows its location on an on-board screen.

• An underwater camera: a vital bit of kit for sneaking snaps of the monster. Make sure it's waterproof.

• A monster-sized fishing net (optional).

Step 3: Collect your evidence

There have been hundreds of sightings of lake monsters. But even serious (and not-so-serious) scientific expeditions haven't managed to catch a monster and bring it back. So how on Earth can you prove your monster actually exists? Monster snaps are great for starters. But you'll need to check they're not fakes. In 1934 a photo taken by a top London surgeon caused a stir when it appeared in a newspaper. It clearly showed the long neck of the Loch Ness monster poking up above the lake. But was this a real monster piccie? Or something much fishier? Years later, the photo turned out to have been a fake all along. The object was actually a plastic tube stuck on top of a toy submarine and not a lake monster at all! Even the lake was a fake.

Horrible Health Warning

So you've scoured the lake with sonar and the evidence is mounting up. In fact, you're 99.99 per cent sure a monster's down there somewhere. But here's a word of warning: don't expect anyone else to believe a word you say. Plenty of people poo-poo the whole idea of lake monsters and reckon monster-hunters are, well, monster raving mad. It's more likely your so-called monster is the wake from a passing boat, a clump of floating waterweeds or a sinister seiche*, they say. They even suggest that patches of sunlight and shadows on the lake water are playing tricks on your eyes. Changed your mind yet?

* Technically speaking, a seiche (say-sh) is a gigantic wave that sloshes up and down in a lake like water in the bathtub. Seiches are set off by strong winds, storms and even earthquakes. (A legend from New Zealand blames seiches on a lake giant breathing in and out.) When an earthquake hit Lisbon in Portugal in 1755, it set off a monster-sized seiche in far-off Loch Ness. Very sloppy, if you ask me.

Monster hide-and-seek

While you're drying out and getting the bits of waterweeds out of your hair, here's the true story of a hunt for the most famous lake monster of all…

It was a balmy summer's afternoon in June 1972. Top American scientist and monster-hunter Dr Robert Rines was sitting contentedly in a cottage on the shore of Loch Ness in Scotland, having tea with his wife and friends. Nothing odd about that, you might think. But this cosy scene was about to be shattered. Seriously shattered. After tea, Dr Rines's friend, Basil Cary, popped outside to smoke his pipe. Seconds later, the others heard a frantic shout…

"Quickly! Come quickly!" Cary yelled. "And bring the binoculars."

Dr Rines rushed out of the house and ran down to the water's edge. Peering through the binoculars, he couldn't believe his eyes. Moving slowly across the loch was a large, round hump, about the size of an upturned boat. Except this was no boring old boat. Through the binoculars, the hump seemed to be covered in rough, grey skin, like an elephant.

Except this was no elephant. As Rines watched in astonishment, the hump changed direction and headed straight towards where he stood. Suddenly, before his eyes, it disappeared into the depths of the lake. What on Earth did the hump belong to? In Rines's mind, there was no doubt. There was only one creature it could be … the mysterious Loch Ness monster.

Later, Rines described that fateful day: "The hair stood up on the back of my neck," he recalled, sighing happily. "I'll never forget it as long as I live. At that moment, I knew there was something in there. I knew it was an animal!"

But was there actually a monster lurking in Loch Ness? Or had the dippy Doc let his monster-sized imagination run away with him? Read on, if you dare…

Monster mania

Loathsome Loch Ness is a ghastly gash across the Scottish countryside, gouged out by ancient glaciers. When the grinding glaciers melted, the steep-sided slash was filled up with icy-cold water. Determined Dr Rines wasn't the first to have his teacups rattled by tales of a monster lurking in the loch's murky depths. For centuries, there had been thousands of chilling rumours about this baffling beast. How's this for starters? In the 6th century, a meandering monk from Ireland saw the head of a hideous monster rearing up out of the loch. The normally mild-mannered monk gave the monster a good telling off and it turned tail and scarpered. Apparently.

ON YER BIKE!

In 1933, a brand-new road was built along the shore which gave a brilliant view over the loch. Soon the newspapers were packed with eyewitness accounts of a monster. But what exactly did the beastly creature look like? Oddly, no two reports could agree. Some people said the beast looked quite like a giant frog. Sort of. Or a huge snail (minus its huge shell). Some counted one hump on its back. Others swore it had seven or more. It was horribly difficult to know who to believe. One thing was certain: monster mania was reaching fever pitch. A curious circus owner even wanted the monster to star in his next show. He offered a whopping reward for the beast and got a monster-sized cage ready. Before long, hundreds of monster-spotters had flocked to Loch Ness, hoping to strike lucky.

One newspaper hired a big-game hunter to track down the monster. And when the hunter found a monster-sized set of footprints on the loch shore, they thought they'd got a sensational scoop. How lucky was that? Plaster casts were made of the footprints and sent to the Natural History Museum in London, where lots of horribly serious scientists tried to work out what on Earth the freaky feet belonged to. Bet you can't guess what they found? The footprints hadn't been formed by a monster at all but by an umbrella stand made from a stuffed hippo foot! Talk about making a monster mistake...

Monster snaps

A few months after his first glimpse of the monster, Dr Rines was back at Loch Ness again. Trouble is, this loathsome loch is horribly deep, dark and freezing cold. And its gloomy waters stretch for miles and miles. Never mind needles and haystacks, trying to find anything in its dismal depths is almost impossible. So this time, our intrepid Doc took along a team of experts and a boatload of high-tech gear. This included sophisticated sonar, flashlights and automatic cameras. The plan was for the sonar to locate the monster, then the cameras would take some snaps as proof.

So did all this costly equipment do the trick? Well, yes ... and no. Incredibly, after weeks of waiting, it seemed the plan had paid off. Early one misty morning, the cameras snapped what looked like a large, diamond-shaped fin about 2 metres long! Could this be a monster's flipper? Or had flaky Rines finally flipped his lid? Other photos followed that seemed to show the head and body of a monster-like creature. It was horribly exciting. But were these photos phoney? Or could they actually be the real deal? As usual, the squabbling scientists couldn't agree about anything...

Some scientists reckoned the photos were genuine and they gave the monster a posh-sounding name. They called it Nessitera rhombopteryx*, after its rhomboid-shaped flipper (a rhomboid is like a squashed rectangle). Try saying that in a hurry. What's more, a debate was even held about the monster in the British Parliament so it seemed the monster was being taken seriously at last. One brave boffin stuck his neck out and suggested the monster must be a plesiosaur, a kind of prehistoric turtle with a long neck. He reckoned it found its way into the loch by swimming from the sea up the River Ness. But other sniffier scientists scoffed at his ideas and said they smelled a monster-sized rat. They pointed out that one of the snaps actually showed a rotting tree stump. OK, so it might look like a monster but only if you screwed your eyes up. Besides, plesiosaurs liked to live in warm, toasty seas. A day or two in the ch-ch-chilly loch and these long-lost reptiles would have frozen to death. Oh and they died out millions of years ago.

*They later discovered that if you rearrange some of the letters in Nessitera rhombopteryx, you get the words "Monster hoax!" Very puzzling.

HOAX? ME?

Return to the lake

Did the squabbling scientists put monster-mad Rines off? No way. But because he was busy doing other things, it was another 25 years before he returned to the loch. This time he brought along a leading sonar expert who specialized in locating hard-to-find underwater objects. Perfect for hunting monsters. Rines also had a brand-new bit of kit called GPS (that's short for Global Positioning System) up his sleeve. The plan was to sweep the loch with sonar and if the sonar picked up a target, he'd use the GPS to pinpoint its exact location. Then a second boat would move in with cameras and capture the whole thing on film. Surely this time they could put the monster mystery to bed? They had just five days to find out. Here's how the Doc might have reported his findings in his daily video diary…

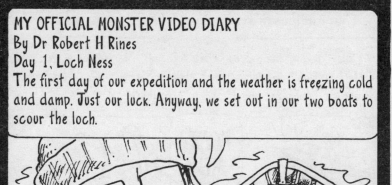

MY OFFICIAL MONSTER VIDEO DIARY
By Dr Robert H Rines
Day 1, Loch Ness
The first day of our expedition and the weather is freezing cold and damp. Just our luck. Anyway, we set out in our two boats to scour the loch.

REC

Everything went swimmingly until water seeped into the cameras and ruined the film. What a blow. We'll have to send for spares. But our hopes were raised when the sonar picked up a big, blob-like shape. Then it disappeared again. Was it the monster playing hide-and-seek? Or was it just soundwaves bouncing off the steep sides of the loch and sending back masses of echoes?

REC

Day 2, Loch Ness (again)
A horribly disappointing day. Today the blinking sonar only picked up a few puny fish. Pah! Looks like Nessie's given us the slip again. But we're not giving up — oh no. I know there's a monster out there somewhere. I can feel it in my bones.
P.S. The new camera hasn't arrived yet. Grrr.

REC

Day 3, Urquhart Bay
At nightfall, I set off with ace photographer Charles Wyckoff in the sonar boat. We decided to concentrate our search on Urquart Bay, the deepest part of the lake. For hours, there was nothing to see. Then, suddenly, there it was on the screen — an object over 5 metres long. Using our trusty GPS, we searched the same area again. If the object was still there, it was most likely a boring old rock or log. If not, it must be moving...

And guess what? Next time we looked, it had gone! All the experts agreed this was no shoal of fish. It looked more like a whale. What we needed now was a photo as proof.

Day 4, Loch Ness (shoreline)

This morning, there was brilliant news. Our new camera had arrived and this beauty is top of the range. It can see further under water and go several hundred metres down, much deeper than the old one. So we're back in action at last, and I for one can't wait for tomorrow when we'll find the monster for sure (I hope).

Day 5, Urquhart Bay (again)

Our last day on the loch and the water was fabulously flat and calm. Perfect for monster-hunting. Armed with our new camera, we set off in the boat. This time, there was a real buzz. Late in the morning, the sonar showed up an object 25 metres down. Then another! Then another! But before the camera could snap them, the wretched things had moved out of range! It was horribly disappointing. Just when we'd got so close to the monster, we'd hit rock bottom again. Never mind. One thing's for certain – I'll be back.

Monster lake fact file

NAME: Loch Ness
LOCATION: Scotland
SIZE: 57 sq km
MAXIMUM DEPTH: 240 metres
MONSTER FACTS:

• Loch is the Scottish word for lake. But the Lake Ness Monster doesn't sound so catchy.

• It's the largest freshwater lake in Britain.

• It lies in a giant crack in the Earth's crust, which was scraped into shape by ancient glaciers. Until the ice melted, 12,000 years ago, the liquid loch was a solid block of ice.

• If you're serious about monster hunting, why not sign up for the Official Loch Ness Monster Fan Club and become an official Nessie fan?

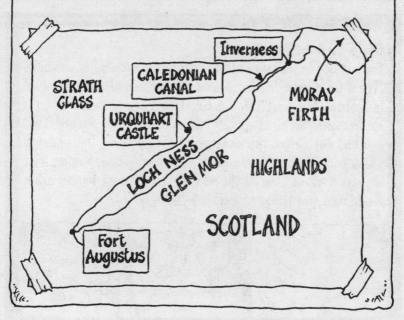

So are scientists any closer to solving the great monster mystery? Until someone catches a real-life monster and brings it back, it's a mystery if lake monsters exist at all. If you haven't spotted a monster yet, you could always try shouting at it. Don't worry about feeling silly. You won't be the only one. The Ogopogo Calling Contest is held every year on Lake Okanagan in Canada. Hundreds of people crowd on to the lakeshore and shout at the tops of their voices. There's a $50 prize for the person who manages to wake the monster up. THINK YOU'D BE IN WITH A SHOUT?

LEAKY LAKES

If you haven't tracked down a lake monster yet, you'd better get your skates on. Monster lakes all over the world are well and truly on their last lap. Some leaky lakes dry up naturally over thousands of years and there's nothing you can do to stop that. But over half the world's loathsome lakes are in deadly danger because of horrible humans. Yep, these lakes are coming under serious strain. (So that's bad luck if you rely on lakes for your drinking water and on lake-living fish for your food, as millions of people do.) But what on Earth are harmful humans doing that's so sickening? You're about to find out.

Four rancid reasons not to go jump in a lake

1 Filthy water. Forget fragrant fresh water. Some lakes are so filthy they've been declared officially DEAD. And others are already in a monster mess. Take Lake Baikal in Siberia. Its once crystal-clear water is being horribly contaminated by waste (dirty water and poisonous chemicals) from a paper factory built on its shore. Each year, the factory pours billions of tonnes of waste into the lake, making the water disgustingly dirty and putting the lake's rare plants and animals at risk.

What's more, the lake's so blooming big it takes 400 years for rivers to replace its water supply. So any perilous pollution hangs around for centuries.

2 Suffocating green scum. In some places, stinking sewage is pumped straight into lakes. And fertilizers and pesticides wash into lakes from farmers' fields, making lakes horribly sick. The sewage and other chemicals get gobbled up by tiny plants called algae. Then these little bloomers grow and grow and grow – until they cover the lake surface in smelly green slime. The smothering slime blocks out sunlight, which other lake plants need to make food. And when it dies and rots, it uses up so much oxygen that fish and other lake creatures suffocate. The slime's not usually hazardous for human swimmers but how would you fancy going paddling in pongy, thick pea soup?

3 Deadly poisonous fish. Fish in thousands of lakes in Scandinavia have been killed by rain that's as acidic as vinegar. But where on Earth does this rancid rain come from? It's actually caused by fumes from cars and factories rising into the air and blowing thousands of miles on the wind. The fumes contain ghastly gases that mix with water vapour and sunlight to make weak but deadly acids, which fall to Earth as rain. Some acid rain falls straight into lakes. Some falls on land and washes into the water, killing fish or making them so poisonous they'd be fatal for people (or other animals) to eat.

4 Bone-dry lake bed. All over the world, people are tapping into monster lakes to supply water for drinking, farming, factories and cities. And it's putting lakes under terrible pressure. Trouble is, it's a vicious circle. Horrible humans need lake water to live, but they're draining some luscious lakes dry and cutting off vital water supplies. Which means there's no lake water for them to use. Take the sorry story of the Aral Sea. So much water's been diverted for farming that the lake has shrunk to a third of its size. We sent roving reporter Blake on a special assignment to investigate…

ARAL SEA 1960

ARAL SEA 1995

I'm here in Central Asia, checking out what's actually happening to the Aral Sea. I'd heard rumours that the lake was shrinking and I wanted to sea, sorry, see for myself. And I'm sorry to say it's true. Over the last 40 years, two thirds of this enormous lake has been drained dry (that's like emptying the whole of Lake Erie and Lake Ontario). So how on Earth did things go so horribly wrong?

Until recently, the salty Aral Sea was the world's fourth-largest lake, covering 68,000 square kilometres. But its fortunes have dipped alarmingly. In the 1960s, colossal canals were built to carry water from the rivers feeding the lake to farmers' fields hundreds of kilometres away. This cuts down the amount of water flowing into the lake to a tenth of what it was. Before long, vast stretches of once water-logged lake had turned into desperate desert. You don't need a fishing boat to pootle about on this bone-dry lake bed. A couple of camels will do nicely. At the same time, the patches of water left behind have become saltier and saltier, spelling disaster for the lake's wildlife. Local fishermen used to catch a staggering 50,000 tonnes of fish a year, but the last fish died out years ago. And the lake's shrunk so mind-bogglingly fast, several fishing ports have been left stranded on the shore.

So what does the future hold for the shrinking sea? Unless something's done to stop the rot, the lake will have vanished completely in 15 to 20 years' time. In the 1990s, some of the lost lake water was topped up by heavy rains. But the leaking lake's future looks bleak. Tragically, the countries around its shores don't seem too bothered about trying to save the Aral Sea. They're too busy squabbling among themselves about getting their fair share of water.

Horrible Health Warning

The water hyacinth is a luscious lake plant with pretty purple flowers. Nothing wrong with that, you might think. Except this blossoming bloomer gets EVERYWHERE, tangling fishing boats in its tendrils and clogging up vital fishing grounds. Unfortunately, this pesky plant's horribly tricky to get rid off. There's no point picking it because it'll grow back double the size in less than a week! Villagers around Lake Victoria tried paying a witch doctor to magic the monstrous weed away. Sadly, it made no difference at all and the weedy witch doctor had to give his money back. But the villagers had got another trick up their sneaky s-leaves. They chucked in bucketloads of tiny beetles called weevils to gobble up the woeful weeds. And guess what? Their plan worked perfectly and the well-fed weevils are still beetling away.

BURP!

A monster future?

But before you get too bogged down, don't worry, it isn't all bad news. All over the world people are working hard to clean up lakes and protect them for the future. Action plans are already up and running on many monster lakes, like Lake Mono in California, USA. For centuries, this little lake lapped along happily and was home to hundreds of lake animals and birds. Then, in the 1940s, the supersized city Los Angeles began piping drinking water from the rivers that fed the lake. The lake's water level dropped alarmingly and things looked gloomy for the wildlife. For years, local people campaigned hard to save their lake and now things are looking up. Water is still allowed to flow into Los Angeles, but much less than before. And the lake's beginning to fill up again. So everybody's happy.

Earth-shattering fact
Officials at an Australian ski resort have come up with an ingenious lake-saving idea. Each year, some 300 million litres of water are taken from lakes to make snow for the ski slopes. Now the plan is to replace this with pee – yes, pee – from the thousands of skiers. It'll be cleaned and turned into snow, leaving the lakes in pee-ce.

So your foul field trip's finally over and it's time to head back home. You've seen enough loathsome lakes to last you a lifetime but you haven't found a long-lost lake monster yet. But hang on just a tick. What on Earth's that sinister shadow lurking in the undergrowth? It's horribly grey and slimy, and it's covered in dank waterweeds. It's coming straight for you… Don't panic, it isn't a mysterious monster. That would be horribly exciting. It's just your soaking-wet geography teacher and it looks as if she's gone and sprung a whole lakeful of leaks…

If you're still interested in finding out more about monster lakes, here are some websites you can check out:

www.worldatlas.com
A list of all the world's lakes with bucketloads of facts and figures to look up for each of them.

www.globalnature.org
An international network dedicated to looking after lakes, their wildlife and people all over the world.

www.nessie.co.uk
A brilliant website for the Loch Ness Monster, with facts, photos and sightings, including sonar contacts.

www.great-lakes.net
Information about the Great Lakes and the dangers facing them, with a brilliant question and answer section.

www.shipwreckmuseum.com
Visit some of the sunken shipwrecks found on the beds of the Great Lakes and find out how they met their watery ends.

www.ramsar.org
The website of the Ramsar Convention, which works to protect the world's wetlands (lakes, rivers, swamps and ponds), with a special feature on "World Wetlands Day".

HORRIBLE INDEX

127